Clyde Coast Connections
Robert Grieves

Choosing *Clyde Coast Connections* as a title gives me virtually unlimited scope to indulge my interests in public transport. Connections related to transport can normally be construed as a link between buses and trains, trains and ferries, buses and buses or any other such combination. Scheduling the arrival of one vehicle or vessel to take place shortly before departure of the other is not as simple as it would appear and most of us have experienced at some time or another the frustration of a disappearing view of the back of a bus or stern of a steamer caused by a missed connection.

My interpretation of the Clyde Coast involves the Firth all the way to Campbeltown in Kintyre and Inveraray on Loch Fyne, one of the many scenic arms of this wonderful waterway. The once famous railway map reproduced on page 2 gives a bird's eye view of the area covered.

Perhaps my own favourite pier for colourful connections was Brodick on Arran, an island at one time served by boats and buses at a variety of villages all around its shores. Even after Brodick became the sole main port it was still a marvellous meeting place for so many small operators, each serving their own patch on the holiday isle.

On Scotland's Clyde Coast there are probably more examples of connections between different forms of public transport than in any other part of the British Isles. This is largely due to the physical features of the area which require ferry services to islands and peninsulas where to drive by road would involve an inordinate amount of time. This can be eased with a less stressful journey by ferry and accordingly large numbers elect to sail over the Firth.

Today's ferry links are only a fraction of former years and the number of piers still in use has dropped dramatically. This gives me an opportunity to illustrate some of the connections once available but now only a memory. Indeed, nostalgia plays a large part in the book, but rightly so I suggest. I suspect these pages will probably appeal in particular to gentlemen of a certain age, simply because they can still identify with much of the content. I hope the illustrations will also spark an interest in others who are not even at an age to recall the events and suitably encourage them to conduct research of their own.

The most interesting connections involve different forms of transport, but this has not precluded my use of many scenes showing buses or steamers on their own in appropriate circumstances. So let's enjoy looking wistfully back over a century and more at a variety of views now only possible through a rose-tinted lens.

My choice of photographs is selective and so there is no attempt to cover every pier on the Clyde Coast. Neither have I attempted to describe all vessels or vehicles, nor indeed any particular period. Some of the content may be described as lacking in photographic merit, although I would argue that these are more than compensated for by their atmosphere. This book is a nostalgic remembrance of happy days spent by bus, train and steamer visiting the wealth of delightful spots on the Clyde and its many arms. I have not, however, contained myself to those parameters and also stray outwith the period of personal recall by including many interesting views from earlier years on the Clyde. I have not set out to be exhaustive, so please do not be annoyed if your favourite vessel or resort is not featured. Please just enjoy my random *pot pourri* of this, that and the other which I trust you will find an interesting selection of scenes on the Clyde and its environs over a century and more.

Acknowledgements

Thanks are due to the following for their contributions of photographs: the British Commercial Vehicle Museum, Alan Brotchie, Charlie Crawford for allowing the use of photographs taken by his father the late David Crawford, the late Morton Hunter and Garry Ward.

Although the text of this book had been completed by Robert by the time of his death, some pieces of information remained to be checked together with the usual pre-publishing process of checking of galley and page proofs. Robert's partner, Sadie Smart (née Moore), managed this process aided by Donald Booth, George Heaney, Lawrence MacDuff, John Newth, John Openshaw and John Sinclair.

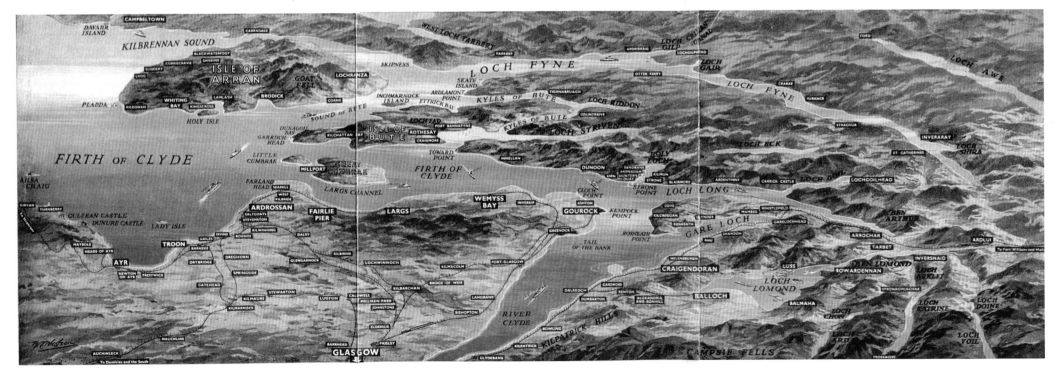

We start our Clyde Coast journey in the heart of the city of Glasgow, appropriately at Broomielaw where so many Glaswegians boarded vessels for the famous sail 'Doon the Watter' to Dunoon, Rothesay or possibly, depending on funds, even further. From the inception of Glasgow's municipal transport system in Victorian times, originally based on horse-drawn and then electric tram cars, citizens were delivered for their day 'Doon the Watter' by Corporation tram or bus. The majority of the north-south tram routes crossed the river by Glasgow (or Jamaica) Bridge which became increasingly congested until King George V Bridge opened. Glasgow was relatively late (December 1924) to introduce municipal buses, largely in response to the huge number of independent bus owners competing against the city trams and the first cross-river Corporation bus service did not commence until November 1927 when service 2 between Knightswood and King's Park was routed across Jamaica Bridge. This was followed by three further important north-south services: 3 (Kelvindale – Mosspark), 4 (Balornock – Drumoyne) and 5 (Muirend – Hope Street, later extended to Knightswood).

This 1926 view of Glasgow Bridge clogged with traffic shows how it carried the majority of cross-river traffic until relieved by the opening of King George V Bridge in 1928. Seen from the bus stance at the western corner of Carlton Place, a wide variety of the small, mainly 14 and 20 seat buses, operated by a multiplicity of independent concerns (some owned only a single vehicle) are visible amongst cars, vans, horse-drawn vehicles and Corporation tramcars. The majority of the buses were on services via Paisley Road West to Paisley and Johnstone and include locally built Albions and Beardmores. Both buses in the foreground are bound for Gourock. GB 3907 on the left, a Yoker-built Halley, was operated in yellow livery by the George Hiring Co. (fleet name Seestu – the old name for Paisley) and owned by Cowan of Johnstone. It was on an interesting route from the city via Paisley, Bishopton, Langbank, Port Glasgow and Greenock. The other is one of several American Reos in the blue Pullman Service fleet of Harold Whatmough of Gourock and ran there via Renfrew and along the south bank of the river. Connections were provided to many places in the 1920s which lack such a service today, remembering of course car ownership at that time was minimal by comparison, thus encouraging bus owners to provide transport over some ingenious routes.

Jumping ahead to the mid-1950s, two Corporation Daimler double deckers await departure time at the service 39 terminus in the then new Pollok housing scheme. Newly delivered in 1955 was Weymann bodied FYS 525 (D70) while FYS 110 (D10) of 1949 was bodied by Northern Coachbuilders of Newcastle-upon-Tyne. Note the continued use of the FYS letters over the years, as Glasgow Corporation had obtained the whole series which was subsequently allocated to all kinds of municipal vehicles.

The terminus in the city was the Broomielaw, which at that time was home to several south side services and extremely useful if connecting for a sail on a steamer down the river, although by this time all pleasure cruises ran from Bridge Wharf on the south bank. The last sailings from Broomielaw had been by *Davaar* and *Dalriada* to Campbeltown but ceased when the Second World War broke out.

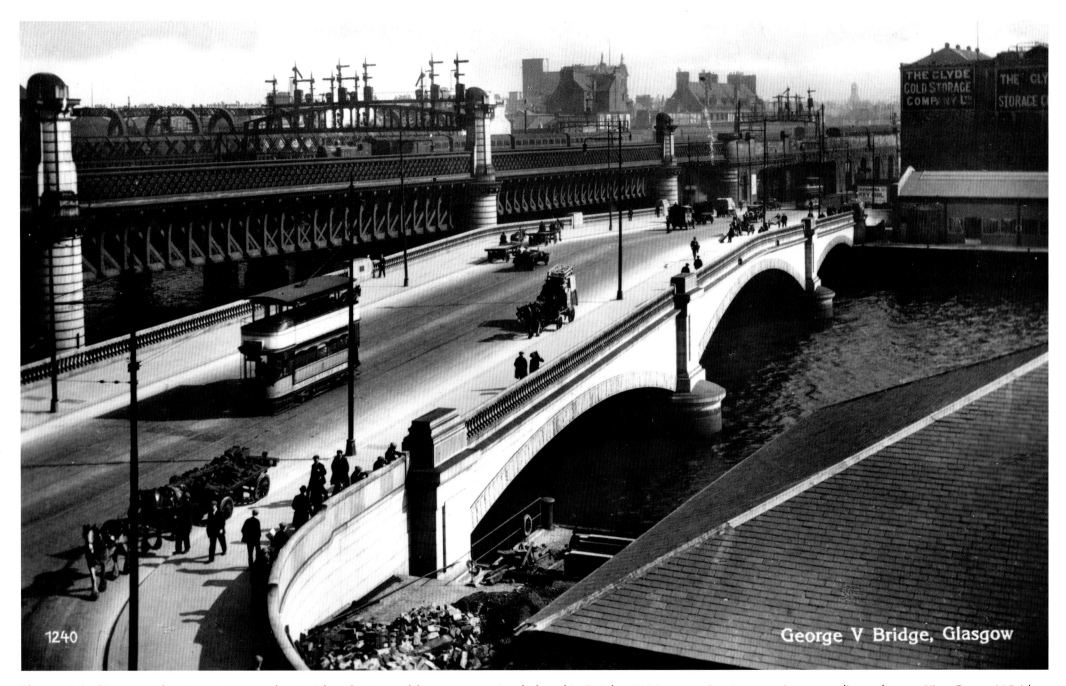

1240

George V Bridge, Glasgow

The municipal transport department was not slow to take advantage of the new cross-river link and in October 1928 appropriate tram services were diverted to use King George V Bridge. This view shows white car 750 on a very quiet bridge with more horse-drawn than motor traffic visible. The tram still has a trolley pole, rather than a bow collector of the type fitted from 1931 onwards. LMS 0-4-4 tank engine 15174 hauls a passenger train towards Central Station beneath the gantry of semaphore signals standing like sentinels against the skyline.

4

Left: A huge order for Leyland Titan double decker buses commenced delivery to Glasgow Corporation in 1928, allowing new services to be introduced all over the city, further encouraging Glaswegians to travel to and from the Clyde Coast via the steamer terminals. A typical example of Glasgow's first fleet of double deckers passes the Corporation Transport head office at the corner of Bath Street and Hope Street shortly after delivery. 99 (GE 2434) is on service 7 which at that time ran between Possilpark and Polmadie, pursued by a tramcar on the white service to Mosspark. Prior to the era of traffic lights, 99 would have been waved through the junction by the helmetted police constable on duty. Note also the once familiar head office clock with the wording 'Tramway Offices'. This was soon to be changed to 'Transport Offices' as the bus fleet steadily grew in importance.

Above: This bird's eye view of King George V Bridge from ten years later shows how convenient it was for travel to the quays of the Broomielaw and Clyde Place, with Central Station visible to the right. On this occasion the bridge is bereft of tramcars and the sole bus is Corporation 524 (BGA 90), a Daimler COG6 model with streamlined bodywork by Weymann, working service 3 to Mosspark via the Empire Exhibition at Bellahouston Park which, with its influx of visitors from near and far, considerably boosted business throughout the city.

Below: A typical scene looking from King George V Bridge in 1952 as *Duchess of Montrose* departs Bridge Wharf in Clyde Place with what appears to be a maximum load on a still summer morning without enough wind to flutter the ensign at her stern. Ahead of the *Duchess*, *Queen Mary II* continues to load passengers for her 11 o'clock cruise to the Kyles of Bute and Tighnabruaich. Across river at the Broomielaw, *Royal Ulsterman* is berthed for the day prior to her evening departure for the overnight sail to Belfast. The final sailing from Bridge Wharf was by *Caledonia* on 14th September 1969.

Right upper & lower: The passenger connection between the city and the Belfast wharf at the Broomielaw was provided by the coaches of David MacBrayne from a pick-up point in St. Enoch Square. Holidaymakers laden with suitcases could not be expected to attempt the lengthy and exhausting walk involved to join *Royal Ulsterman* or *Royal Scotsman*. The routine was for MacBrayne crews on the daily summer service from Glasgow to Inverness (they changed over at Kinlochleven by swapping vehicles) to work overtime by manning the steamer shuttles. In this early 1960s scene, 178 (UGB 428) of 1958, the first of many Duple (Midland) Donington bodied AEC Reliance coaches in the MacBrayne fleet, awaits intending customers while 45 (WGG 634) pulls up behind. Both display 'Belfast Steamer' destinations on the front window. Coincidentally the advert visible on the British Railways hoarding offers cheap travel on the rival service to Ireland, with special day excursions via Stranraer to Larne at 54/- and Belfast 56/-. *Royal Ulsterman* was withdrawn towards the end of the 1967 season and replaced by *Scottish Coast* which continued to run in tandem with *Royal Scotsman* until early 1968, when the latter was also withdrawn after the introduction of the car ferry *Lion* on the daylight service between Ardrossan and Belfast. The Burns and Laird Line's Belfast connections from Glasgow (Lancefield Quay) ended in 1969, and the 'Derry boat (usually *Lairds Loch*), three years earlier.

St. Enoch Square was also the terminal point for connecting coaches to and from Glasgow Airport (Renfrew, and later Abbotsinch) and Prestwick Airport. Three 1950 AEC Regals of Lowland Motorways' fleet line up awaiting business in the mid-1950s, with Duple-bodied GGG 875 in the centre. Fore and aft are HGE 796 and 797 which, despite being exactly the same age, convey a younger appearance with their full-fronted Burlingham coachwork. Lowland, whose office was in Buchanan Street and whose garage was in Shettleston, sold out to SMT in 1958. As Scottish Omnibuses, SMT continued to operate the air connections for a period before transferring the work to sister company Western SMT, as the service was more economically run from its Inchinnan depot, which was in close proximity to the airport. The three contemporary adverts for Camp Coffee, Palethorpes' Sausages and Barr's Iron Brew (before the spelling change to Irn Bru) are another instant reminder of the fifties. Each was to be seen virtually everywhere in Scotland at the time.

REGULAR AIR SERVICES FROM GLASGOW

| TO BELFAST | TO CAMPBELTOWN | TO ISLAY |
| Return £3 Single £2 | Return £2 Single £1:5 | Return £3 Single £2 |

MIDLAND AND SCOTTISH AIR FERRIES LTD.

COMPANY OFFICES

GLASGOW RENFREW AERODROME TEL. 135-136 (RENFREW) · BELFAST GRAND CENTRAL HOTEL TEL. 7090 (BELFAST) · ISLAY DUICH AERODROME
CAMPBELTOWN STRATH FIELD AERODROME TEL. 183 CAMPBELTOWN · LIVERPOOL HOOTON PARK AERODROME TEL. 197 HOOTON

Above: Prior to the Second World War, Scottish Airways provided flight connections from Renfrew Airport to a variety of west coast and island destinations. This smart Duple-bodied Bedford coach, AYS 774, was purchased in 1937 to provide a convenient link for passengers between the airport and the city.

This scene in July 1965 at Renfrew Airport shows that connections could not have been much closer between the flights and the linking buses from Glasgow Air Terminal at St. Enoch Square. This was the final year of operations from Renfrew, before transfer to Abbotsinch in 1966. In those almost forgotten times of minimal security and much less red tape, the buses would drive alongside the planes to deliver their passengers, who had already checked in at the city terminal. Destinations were set for the appropriate flight, in this instance Birmingham, on Western's Inchinnan-based IL 2038 (CAG 453C), a new Leyland Leopard with Alexander Y-type bodywork, passing Handley Page Herald G-APWD, leased to BEA for service in Scotland, and delivered in May 1962. It was mainly used on the Renfrew – Campbeltown – Islay services until its withdrawal at the end of October 1966.

Clyde Port Authority's *Ferry No. 1* sets out on its voyage from the Broomielaw at Elliot Street to the Tradeston side of the river during a particularly quiet time of evening. This was not always so, of course, as large numbers of workers used this vessel to reach their places of employment along the dockside or perhaps at the Scottish Co-operative Wholesale Society headquarters in Morrison Street, seen against the skyline complete with its concrete statue of Light and Life atop the dome.

The Kingston Bridge takes shape in 1969 as *Queen Mary II* sails stern first upriver to her overnight berth at Bridge Wharf after completing her popular daily 11 o'clock cruise to Tighnabruaich.

Right: Assisted by the tug *Thunderer*, a cargo ship is led past Yorkhill Quay. This scene looks upriver, with Yorkhill Basin, Glasgow's haven for Anchor Line shipping in the 1950s and 1960s, on the left. Against the skyline the multi-storey Queen Mother Hospital is taking shape at Yorkhill.

Below: Down the river were the graving docks at Govan, which were not quite visible on the sail from the city. They were used by several steamer companies to prepare their vessels for the summer season. On this occasion the North British Railway's paddle steamer *Waverley* of 1899 was undergoing treatment and this view from 1908 emphasises her sleek lines.

The Govan/Partick Ferry, one of the numerous cross-river connections which survived into the 1960s. This late Victorian view, looking north towards the mouth of the River Kelvin, shows D & W Henderson's yard to the left, with the Pointhouse yard of A & J Inglis to the right. Visible beyond the ferry is *Waverley*, newly launched and fitting out. The site for the new Glasgow Transport Museum, due to open in 2011, is to the right of the mouth of the Kelvin.

The unmistakable tower of Glasgow University looks down on this 1950s view taken from the Govan side at Water Row towards the approaching vessel arriving from Ferry Road, Partick. Vauxhall and Hillman cars await at the Govan side.

Queen Mary II returning upriver to Bridge Wharf after her daily cruise through the Kyles. Fussy little *Ferry No. 5* has just bustled across the river towards Whiteinch from Linthouse. The huge Meadowside Granary complex and Merkland's Lairage and abbatoir (both now gone) are visible on the north bank of the Clyde as are Fairfield's cranes on the opposite side. As a small boy returning home on the *Lairds Loch* or *Lairds Glen* after a holiday in County Donegal, I recall a feeling of annoyance if our vessel called in at this wharf to discharge cattle. It seemed to take forever when I was desperate to get back home.

Renfrew Ferry was formerly located on the King's Inch, about half a mile east of its present site, moving to today's position in the late 1700s. The first steam powered chain ferry, dating from 1868, was replaced in 1897 by the one shown here, built by McKnight of Ayr. She was purchased in 1911 from the Renfrew Harbour Trust by the Clyde Navigation Trust, who continued ownership of the ferries until formation of the Clyde Port Authority in 1966. Despite withdrawal and replacement by a further steam ferry in 1912, she lingered as a spare for both the Renfrew and Erskine crossings until 1936 when she was sold for service at Kessock, Inverness but instead was scrapped as she was too large to manoeuvre through the locks of the Caledonian Canal. This scene from the Renfrew side around 1900 looks across to Yoker before construction of the Clyde Valley Power Station. At that time almost all traffic was horse-drawn, with motor vehicles still in their infancy. Pedestrian traffic was considerable, with shipyards and factories on both sides of the Clyde providing trade for the cross-river connections.

A 1949 scene from *Queen Mary II* showing the fourth and final steam ferry at the Renfrew shore. She had been built locally by Fleming & Ferguson in 1935 on the River Cart at Paisley and was the regular vessel until replacement by the last chain ferry, diesel-electric powered, in 1952 which was also built by Fleming & Ferguson. The 1935 vessel survived as spare for both Erskine and Renfrew until the demise of the vehicle crossing in 1984. Visible in this photo are reminders of my schooldays haunts including Paton's Tower Garage (named after the huge electricity pylon straddling their premises), and the Paisley & District Daimler double decker at the Ferry terminus on the short run from Paisley shared at that time with Paton, Cunningham of Paisley and Ferguson of Renfrew (Victor). Nor do I forget Coia's Cafe, just beyond the tower, and Robertson's shop next to the historic Ferry Inn. It was in Robertson's many years later that, as a bus driver working variously with Cunningham, Paton, McGill and Western SMT (you could pick and choose in these days), I enjoyed many teas, coffees and snacks paid for, as was tradition, by my conductress. All these establishments were particularly busy for the few minutes before and after the arrival of the ferry from the Yoker side, when passengers from the frequent trams and buses crowded in to make their purchases. Visible on the ferry are Albion and Seddon lorries, while a Bedford lorry followed by a Vauxhall Wyvern drive down the cobbled slip to board.

The unknown photographer on board *Queen Mary II* this summer day in 1949 as she sailed down the river also snapped this scene as she passed Bull's Metal Works at Yoker, looking up the river past Yarrow's Scotstoun Shipyard towards the city. From the stern a father and son look down at the churning waters of the Clyde, which at that time was not too clean. Just looking at the photo reminds me of the less than delightful smell in such situations. I would not describe it as dreadful as it did have a certain repugnant charm (for strange souls like myself) which I suppose will forever be connected with a day 'Doon the Watter' on the oozing river section. The situation has improved considerably since then, to the extent that salmon are now regular visitors.

Renfrew Ferry was served by the electric cars of Paisley District Tramways from 1904 and subsequently by those of Glasgow Corporation Transport after the Paisley company sold out in 1923. This mid-1950s scene at the ferry terminus shows car 909 departing for Paisley and Glenfield, with the conductress appropriately changing the destination in that precarious manoeuvre on a Standard car which virtually involved hanging upside down from the window to wind the screen. At the end of the track is Coronation tram 1279, which will depart in seven minutes for Lochfield Road. A Western SMT Daimler is parked at the Paisley bus stop, while the spare ferry can be seen moored in Renfrew's own little river, the Pudzeoch, where it joins the Clyde.

The view from the ferry in the 1950s when queues such as this were commonplace. Vehicle traffic, headed by an Austin Princess limousine, lines up to reach the Yoker shore, while a service 28 Corporation Standard tramcar loads for Paisley and Elderslie.

I obtained my first camera at primary school, by swapping for some now forgotten treasure. It was of the well-remembered (by those of a certain age) Kodak Brownie box type, activated by a lever. After having pressed it into position, the next photo was taken by returning it in the opposite direction, an unwitting cause of many infuriating double exposures. Fortunately an appropriate birthday and a sympathetic father came to the rescue with an upmarket model of the same make, but with fewer frustrations. Improvements over the years kept me satisfied and now, like most others, I have "gone digital" although believe that a really good print from the pre-digital age is still preferable. Even as a schoolboy I tried to capture my transport scenes "on service" if possible and better still with some background with which one could easily identify. This was very important for someone such as me who was too lazy or, as I'd rather think, too busy, to catalogue photographs, which I've regretted ever since. A picture tells a story and if that picture has been taken in a depot yard close against the bus/loco or whatever, as sadly so many have been, then there is very little story to tell. Even a background road sign or advertising hoarding can help, especially many years later when such extras enhance the general interest.

This 1982 view of Renfrew Ferry, two years before withdrawal of the chain ferry, shows the head of the traffic queue and two buses on the local service to Paisley. Connections between Paisley and Renfrew Ferry were particularly good, with a bus approximately every four minutes provided by Western SMT, Cunningham of Paisley, Paton of Renfrew, and McGill of Barrhead. Similar frequent connections could be found on the north bank of the river at Yoker, where Central SMT and Glasgow Corporation provided frequent links to Clydebank and to the city. TDS 612R, a 1977 Leyland National in the red and grey colours of McGill is about to leave on a Saturday duty through Paisley to Barrhead, a service started by Paisley District Tramways in 1906 and continued by Glasgow Corporation trams until the line was closed over the section between Glenfield and Cross Stobs in 1949. Western's Leyland Leopard served Paisley and the Glenburn housing estate. On this occasion, note how the approaching ferry almost reaches road level; extremely high tides often brought flooding to this low-lying area of Renfrew.

18

Since the demise of the navy blue vehicle ferry on 31st May, 1984, the cross-river connection between Renfrew and Yoker has lost lots of character. I can still recall the clanking of the chains and the strange combination of smells, which seemed like a mixture of oil and river pollution, on my way across to what a small schoolboy always regarded as another world on the north side. Over the river, trams (the Kilmarnock Bogies) were unlike those on the Renfrew side and also different types of buses (Central SMT) added further mystery on forays to the far shore. The replacement passenger ferries, *Renfrew Rose* and *Yoker Swan*, were soulless in comparison since they no longer catered for cars and commercials (apart from an emergency vehicle if required). Initially painted in the corporate orange of Strathclyde Transport, they sail today in the current carmine and cream colours of Strathclyde Passenger Transport. One redeeming feature is that a reminder of the old chain ferry can still be enjoyed since 'Renfrew' is now berthed in the city as a floating restaurant and entertainment centre. [Since the original text was written, SPT has handed over the operation of the service to a private company using smaller ferries.]

THE CLYDE AT RENFREW FERRY, RENFREW.

Apart from its better known cross-river connection, Renfrew could also boast its own wharf a little downstream from the ferry at the terminus of the Paisley-Renfrew railway line. Pleasure steamers from the city called here *en route* to Kirn, Dunoon, Innellan and Rothesay providing a link which was never reinstated after loss of the wharf during the Clydebank Blitz of 1941. This scene from 1924 shows the paddle steamer *Isle of Arran* slowing to call at Renfrew, with a glimpse of vessels on the stocks at Clydebank beyond. The cranes are in the local shipyards at Simons and Lobnitz, next door neighbours who specialised in building dredgers, amalgamating in 1959 but inevitably now closed like most of the other yards. During the Second World War, Lobnitz successfully designed and built the Mulberry Harbours or Churchill's Piers for use on beaches.

Returning to the 19th century, this scene shows the demise of what had been an important transport connection for freight and passengers by canal between Glasgow, Paisley and Johnstone. Originally surveyed by Thomas Telford and planned to go all the way to Ardrossan, in fact Johnstone was the limit reached on opening in 1810, from where it went no further. Boats carrying 120 passengers initially took two hours to make the journey between Glasgow and Paisley but by 1832 lighter vessels drawn by two horses and carrying 100 passengers did the trip in half the time. Around this time, small boats carried passengers down the Cart from Paisley to join the steamers plying on the Clyde. The illustration shows a group of prominent Paisley businessmen gathered on board what was apparently the final excursion on the canal in 1882. The Glasgow and South Western Railway Company then had it drained to provide the track bed for its route between Glasgow, Crookston, Paisley and Johnstone, known to this day as the 'Canal line' and now terminating in Paisley.

Overleaf: As a 'Buddie' I must be forgiven the indulgence of including my home town. Immediately, of course, I hear you query its Clyde connections, but it has a direct link via the few remaining miles of the River White Cart before it joins the Clyde, along with the Black Cart, at Inchinnan. In distant Victorian times there was a passenger steamer connection between Paisley and the Clyde Coast. Even today the occasional small sailing boat takes a tremulous trip, usually simply from curiosity, under the bridge at Inchinnan to reach as far as the old Carlile (*sic*) Quay near the Sneddon. We must not forget our own shipbuilding yards, famously specialising in the construction of dredgers; the last of these, Fleming & Ferguson's, closed in 1968.

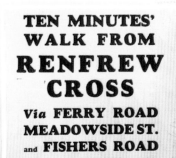

THE **BEST VIEW** OF THE **CUNARDER** ON THE STOCKS IS FROM THE **RENFREW SHORE**

TRAVEL BY GLASGOW

CORPORATION TRANSPORT

534

TEN MINUTES' WALK FROM **RENFREW CROSS** *Via* FERRY ROAD MEADOWSIDE ST. and FISHERS ROAD

Join Renfrew Tram in Hope St.

Above: Not slow to respond to any possibility of extra revenue, Glasgow Corporation Transport Department advertised its connections by tram from the city to Renfrew from where passengers could walk to enjoy seeing the new giant Cunarder being built at John Brown's Clydebank Yard from 1934 to 1936. The best views were obtainable from the south shore and involved catching the car to Renfrew Cross and either walking from there or a further much shorter tram journey by changing to the Ferry car from Paisley to Meadowside Street. The walk commenced from there to see what was then known as '534' on the stocks. She was, of course, to become the 73,000 ton *Queen Mary*, sailing as such from Clydebank to the Tail of the Bank on 24th March, 1936, when citizens again were encouraged to travel by tram either to Renfrew or Dalmuir West to enjoy the spectacle. Similar trips could be made later in the 1930s to view '552' or *Queen Elizabeth* at the same yard. A variety of steamer excursions from Bridge Wharf also catered for the tourist traffic, especially in the boom season of 1938 during the time of the Empire Exhibition. The Caledonian Steam Packet Co., for instance, advertised hourly trips for one shilling from 9.30 a.m. to 7.30 p.m. Reproduced is a typical GCT advertising poster of the mid-1930s, specially shaped to conform with the curve of the tramcar windows.

Right: 20th September, 1967, saw *Duchess of Hamilton* on a special sailing to Rothesay Dock at Clydebank to allow spectators to view the launching of *Queen Elizabeth 2*. And just look at these 1960s saloons! From the left I can recognise an Austin Cambridge van (with the added interest of a good Glasgow registration number GGG 254C of 1965), Ford Zephyr, Vauxhall Velox, Vauxhall Victor, BMC 1100, Humber Super Snipe, and MGB.

The other well-known Clyde chain ferry was that at Erskine, made redundant on the opening of Erskine Bridge in 1971. Coach operators on both sides of the river found it a valuable shortcut avoiding Glasgow when routing their tours. For example this late 1940s scene shows two coaches heading home to Ayrshire after a day excursion to Oban. Driving up the slip on the Erskine shore is BAG 516, a 1946 Duple-bodied AEC Regal which was the first new coach delivered post-war to Dodds of Troon. On board the ferry is a Bedford OB type coach.

In the early 1920s, prior to the grouping in 1923 of the railway companies in the west of Scotland to form the London, Midland and Scottish Railway, competition was still at a high level. Prospective passengers were all important and steamer facilities from Greenock to the Clyde Coast resorts were served by two rival companies, each jealously guarding its own custom. Both these scenes date from around 1920, the upper showing a Glasgow and South Western Railway train crossing the Gryffe Viaduct in Bridge of Weir *en route* for Kilmacolm and Greenock (Princes Pier) where a seamless connection was made to company steamers. The locomotive was of the Manson 4-4-0 Greenock Bogie type, hauling a train of late Victorian coaches. Princes Pier Station had been built by the G&SW in order to capture a larger slice of the coastal traffic. Passengers using the line from Glasgow (St. Enoch) via Paisley (Canal) and Kilmacolm could therefore step from train to steamer at Princes Pier, whereas the rival Caledonian Railway route from Glasgow Central to Greenock (and later to Gourock) was more direct via Paisley Gilmour Street and Bishopton, but the downside was the walk between station and pier in Greenock. This scene at Bishopton Station shows Caley loco 721 in the company's attractive blue livery *en route* from Gourock to Glasgow. The original station building still stands at Bishopton today, but the signal box has gone and the passenger footbridge replaced.

If arrival in Port Glasgow was by train in the 1940s or 50s then on leaving the station one would almost invariably find a Greenock Motor Services bus on one of several frequent local services. On a sunny summer morning in 1949 Guy Arab/Weymann ASD 757 awaits custom for Greenock and will travel past numerous still busy shipyards including once familiar names such as Lithgow's, Hamilton's, George Brown's (Garvel Yard) and Scotts.

At the Greenock Esplanade end of its run from Port Glasgow, locally registered Guy Arab VS 4651 of 1947 with Guy's own attractive bodywork, pauses near Princes Pier before returning. Until 1952 Princes Pier was still in regular use for pleasure steamers, and passenger trains continued to use this station until 1959.

Left: Its very simplicity makes this dramatic advert for the Anchor Line extremely effective. It appeared in 1931 when Transatlantic connections from the Clyde were still very much in operation and features *Transylvania*, completed in 1925 by the Fairfield Shipbuilding and Engineering Co. at Govan. Her career ended prematurely when she was torpedoed off Ireland in 1940 while on duty as an armed merchant cruiser.

Overleaf: The River Clyde really widens out to become the Firth as we sail on past the 'Tail of the Bank' and slip past Cardwell Bay to berth at Gourock. Here again, good connections by bus were provided by Greenock Motor Services along the riverside corridor between Ashton and Woodhall, linking with other GMS routes to upper Inverclyde. Gourock Pierhead was the local operational hub, with a number of buses terminating here, including Western SMT's Glasgow services seen in 1949 at the 'through' bus stop outside the post office. Double decker BSD 409 was a Northern Counties-bodied AEC Regent while BAG 156 was a Brush-bodied AEC Regal, both based at Inchinnan Depot which operated both the Glasgow – Renfrew – Gourock service and the Glasgow – Paisley – Bridge of Weir – Gourock route. These were usually differentiated by crews as the 'low road' and 'high road' services. Western's small depot in Gourock, a satellite of Inchinnan, shared this work.

THE GREENOCK MOTOR SERVICES COMPANY
(INCORPORATED BY ACT OF PARLIAMENT)
FORMERLY THE GREENOCK AND PORT-GLASGOW TRAMWAYS COMPANY
Offices: DELLINGBURN, GREENOCK. *Telephones*: 1151, 1152

Frequent services of Omnibuses are operated from Greenock to the adjoining Burghs of Port-Glasgow and Gourock, and throughout Greenock. Special facilities are offered to Workers between their homes and the Docks, Industrial and Business Centres.
During the Summer, Services along the shores of the Firth of Clyde, to Gourock, Ashton, and Lunderson Bay, and to the Hills, Moors, and Golf Course, are operated by a fleet of modern buses.

Private Hires for Theatres, Cinemas, Sporting Events and Excursion Parties arranged at Moderate Charges

Facing the camera, and only a few months old is VS 4868, a Leyland PD1 with poorly constructed bodywork by Strachan of Acton which, like all other similar buses in the fleet, was rebodied by Eastern Coach Works at Lowestoft after less than four years in service. It is about to leave the 'local' stop to turn and absorb the queue seen patiently waiting for Greenock, Port Glasgow and Woodhall. Behind it is VS 4349, one of many wartime utility Guy Arabs in the GMS fleet, this one with Weymann bodywork similar to that seen on page 27. November 1949 saw the demise of Greenock Motor Services which had been a subsidiary company of Western SMT for several years and was then totally acquired by them. Between the buses and Cardwell Bay is Gourock Station, terminus of the line from Glasgow, with the pier immediately beyond, combining to give Gourock excellent connections by road, rail and steamer.

Hiccups happen. Inevitably occasional disruption takes place to transport services due to any one of a variety of circumstances. This situation occurred in 1970 when disruption on the railway line required the substitution of buses to maintain services. These were provided by Paton Bros. of Renfrew and seen here on Gourock Pier are former Birch Brothers of London Leyland Tiger Cub WXR 52, with Leyland Titan PD2s FJF 168, FDJ 820 and EO 9064, previously in the municipal fleets of Leicester, St. Helens and Barrow-in-Furness respectively.

Looking across the bow of *Queen Mary II* towards Kilcreggan on the far shore in July 1965, we see Gourock Pier in happier days. *Caledonia* forges away in a froth of Firth water bound for Rothesay on a day excursion. The first vessel thus named for the Caledonian Steam Packet Company Ltd. had been retired in 1933, followed by this second Denny-built paddler in 1934. During the Second World War as HMS *Goatfell* she achieved distinction as a minesweeper and also acted as an escort ship, returning in 1946 to Clyde Coast sailings after reconditioning at her Dumbarton builders. There is certainly no mistaking *Caledonia* as a paddler from this angle, but because her paddle boxes were streamlined in an effort to appear more modern in the 1930s, she could be mistaken for a turbine when viewed broadside. Berthed at the top end of the pier is the Dunoon car ferry *Bute* while prominent among the vehicles on the pier is a Morris J4 type van in Scottish Daily Express livery, having delivered newspapers to the ships' shops.

Gourock Pier from a similar angle in 2009, looking this time from aboard *Jupiter* as she sails for Dunoon. Sadly the pier today has an air of neglect formerly unknown. *Seabus* is a recent addition to the small Clyde Marine Motoring fleet and was built in Plymouth for the Gourock – Kilcreggan – Helensburgh service as successor to the veteran *Kenilworth*, built in 1936 and which remained in occasional service until 2009. Visible in the now roofless station is a Juniper train in Strathclyde Transport livery providing the connecting rail link to Paisley and Glasgow.

SD 5508 of 1921 was one of the many ever popular and economic Model T Fords of the period. This was a left-hand-drive version, seen at Wemyss Bay Station with proud owner Alf Davis of Largs in the driving seat. Alf had previously driven for Scottish Transport in Largs (the predecessor of Western SMT) before starting his own business running services from Largs, Wemyss Bay, and Fairlie. With no rail connection between Wemyss Bay and Largs, Davis served additional demand for buses despite Dunlop of Greenock operating regular Greenock to Largs services, both via Gourock and the Kip Valley. Thankfully the delightful station buildings at Wemyss Bay have largely escaped change and present the same attractive appearance today.

THE PIER, WEMYSS BAY

D 5509

Wemyss Bay Pier in 1960 with the car ferry *Cowal* of 1954. Designed and built as a side-loading vessel by the Ailsa Yard at Troon, she remained in this condition throughout her career, which ended when alteration to the piers at Wemyss Bay and Rothesay during the late 1970s allowed side and end loading. Car ferry services to Millport also operated from Wemyss Bay and seen awaiting boarding is GYS 493, a Bedford 'O' type lorry delivering soft drinks for Moore's 'Sunfresh' of Bridgeton.

One of *Cowal*'s two sisters was *Bute*, also delivered in 1954 as a side loader and built by Ailsa. A newer ferry of the same name, built in Poland in 2005, is seen here bows on as she approaches Wemyss Bay. McGill's of Greenock provided Dennis Dart N504 KCD for the connection to Greenock via the Kip Valley.

Briefly, in 1983-84, Wemyss Bay was the terminus of a strange service run by Western Scottish on an express basis from Glasgow, calling at certain points only *en route*. These journeys did not link with the Rothesay steamer; passengers on the approaching ferry *Saturn* would therefore have had to use the train in the adjacent station or step outside to join the Greenock or Largs bus. On this occasion, Western provided Alexander-bodied Seddon 962 (DSD 962V) in the black, white and grey livery. Cityliner was a relatively short-lived logo used on longer express services before Citylink was formed.

L 2109 The Bay and Pier, Largs.

Largs in 1938 with the paddler *Mercury* steaming in an arc across the bay towards the pier. She was built for the LMS-controlled Caledonian Steam Packet Co. at Fairfield's yard in 1934 but soon after commencing war service work she sank in 1940. At the pierhead is the LMS booking office and waiting room where one of the posters advertises rail excursions to the Empire Exhibition. Largs, like myself, has close links with Brisbane, Queensland, which in turn bonds me to both, as I drove buses in that sub-tropical Australian city for a few years.

Left: Ten years later at the same spot, XS 6463 was a new Leyland Titan PD2 bodied by Northern Counties of Wigan, loading passengers for Young's flagship frequent service via the Haylie Brae to Paisley and Glasgow. Young's Bus Service of Paisley with its attractive yellow (later orange) livery had operated to Largs since the late 1920s and also inaugurated the Largs local service as a summer only operation in 1931.

Below: A further jump of a decade to 1958 at Largs pierhead with three former YBS double deckers lined up outside Castleson's Moorings Restaurant to await return customers to the city. In the red and cream colours of Western SMT, the first two are all-Leyland PD2s of 1950 in the XS 6901-10 series while the Northern Counties-bodied Guy Arab of 1945-46 to the rear was probably one of the XS 5709-18 batch. Virtually every man wears a bunnet. The almost obligatory trench coat, either worn or carried over the arm, was a common accessory against the elements, perceived or otherwise, on the Clyde Coast.

Right: Going back to 1912, Largs pierhead presented a more Spartan appearance with fewer buildings. Even then, however, it was the terminus for the few basic bus services which operated from the town, which was gaining popularity as a good destination for a day out. The two seen here were both Albions owned by McKerrow's West Coast Motor Services and served north to Wemyss Bay. SB 36 in the foreground dated from 1906 and was originally owned by Crosher of Dunoon before its sale to McKerrow. It later ran for MacKay of Largs and Scottish General Transport. Sailing past in the Firth is the majestic *Queen Alexandra*.

Below: Approaching Largs Pier around 1902 is the Caledonian Steam Packet Co.'s *Marchioness of Breadalbane* of 1890, built at John Reid's Port Glasgow yard in the days when it would have been simply unthinkable to have a vessel constructed anywhere other than on the Clyde.

Western SMT Bristol Lodekka 1809 (VCS 363) labours up the steep gradient and severe bends of the Haylie Brae in the 1970s *en route* from Largs to Glasgow. When Young's Bus Service of Paisley pioneered this run, it offered an alternative to the circuitous rival rail journey via Kilwinning and Ardrossan or the equally lengthy road trip via Gourock and the coast which was favoured by other bus companies at the time rather than negotiate the hazards of the Haylie which they considered unsafe. YBS persevered and their next victory was permission from the traffic commissioners to operate double deckers on the route. Western SMT acquired the business in 1951 and continued to operate services to Glasgow from Largs and from West Kilbride (Seamill in summer) from their depots at Johnstone and Largs.

On a personal level I have always had an affinity with YBS and Western SMT. On leaving school I started work with Western in the former Young's head office in Gordon Street, Paisley. In the intervening years I probably worked for as many fifty bus firms, ranging from a day's casual driving to a further fifteen year spell with Western at Inchinnan, and not forgetting a variety of interesting operators on the other side of the world when I lived in Australia during the 1970s.

Apart from Young's Bus Service between Largs and Glasgow via the Haylie Brae, the longer and earlier established route via Renfrew and the coast road was also an option for travellers. Since the railway to Largs was indirect via Kilwinning, Ardrossan and Fairlie, the LMS railway established their own bus service via Renfrew in the late 1920s, initially purchasing Whatmough's Pullman Service of Gourock and then Ferguson's Victoria Pullman of Renfrew, both later incorporated into the Western SMT company. A fleet of Albion saloon buses was used, all registered at LMS headquarters in Derby with CH or UR registration numbers. The Glasgow end of the route was North Drive, the approach ramp to St. Enoch Station, where Albion CH 7926 is seen in the 1930s. This terminus continued in use for the 'low road' services to Gourock and Largs until Anderston Bus Station opened in 1971.

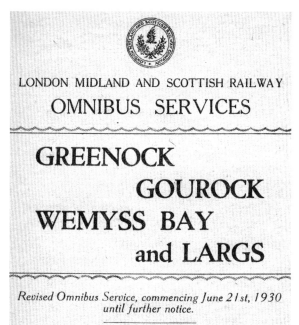

Appropriately the terminus in Largs was outside the entrance to the railway station in Main Street. Railway bus operations were relatively short-lived, with the Largs services passing to Western SMT in 1932 along with the LMS bus garage in Allan Park Street. Seen outside Largs Station in the mid-1930s is one of several new Leyland Tiger TS7T types allocated to the former railway services and finished in the attractive black and white Western livery. The equally smart crews wore boots and leggings at this time enhanced by white-topped caps for summer.

Sunshine, palm trees, bright flower gardens. It must be the Mediterranean, possibly Majorca, but hang on though, that bus looks too familiar. Yes, it's First (Glasgow) Wright Eclipse Gemini-bodied Volvo B7TL SF07 FCZ and it happens to be Largs, not Larnaca. First Bus was one of many companies over the years to try operations between Glasgow and Largs. Like so many others it proved unviable. The attempt lasted for little more than a year, reducing from daily provision to weekends only, prior to permanent withdrawal in late August 2009 when this view was captured on the final Saturday of service. Currently a regular link is provided on this route by McGill's of Greenock, while Peter Harte of Gourock operates a popular connection from Largs to Braehead Shopping Centre via the Haylie Brae. The inland service route via the Haylie Brae and Kilbirnie is served by Arriva, although curtailed to Paisley. [It has since been extended]

Travelling by bus down the coast from Largs was the territory of the aptly named Clyde Coast Services for over half a century. This was a co-operative organisation based in Saltcoats similar to A1 Service, from which CCS had broken away. Seen in the early 1950s at the Saltcoats end of the route from Largs is EWJ 277 a former Sheffield Corporation all-Leyland Titan new in 1938 and one of several secondhand deckers in the smart silver and blue fleet. As a small boy travelling on a double decker my preferred position was perhaps naturally top deck front. If that was not possible then I'd head for the seat behind the driver from where I could look into his cab and observe. Sometimes the bus had one of those wonderful circular Clayton heaters on the bulkhead which served me as a pretend steering wheel, no doubt to the annoyance of others who were not too keen on my aural version of gear changes.

En route from Largs to Saltcoats in the late 1950s is ASD 568, a 1944 utility Guy Arab bodied by Massey of Wigan and owned by CCS member McGregor of Saltcoats. It has just passed a Western SMT Daimler in the village of Fairlie on the lengthy Kilmarnock – Largs – Greenock service. From Fairlie, steamers sailed to Arran and Kintyre in connection with trains from Glasgow and Paisley until closure of the pier in 1972.

Three paddlers seen making a splash at Seamill!!! This would have been the shock horror headline describing such an event in the *Daily Star* but I couldn't resist using it. No sign of *Jeanie Deans* or *Talisman* nor, indeed, any other paddle steamer since the description refers to the three specimens of manhood enjoying a paddle along the Seamill shore in 1935, reminding me more of a Charles Atlas advertisement (the 'before' part, that is). This was always a popular stretch of sandy shoreline but in those days motorists appeared to have less respect for their cars, driving them on the beach regardless of salt water and sand. Young's Bus Service of Paisley extended their Glasgow – West Kilbride route to Seamill during the summer season, a practice continued by Western SMT after the YBS takeover.

A busy early Edwardian scene at Saltcoats with a train from Glasgow having arrived at what at that time was the Glasgow and South Western Railway's station. Onward connections at this date were by horse-drawn cabs from the station forecourt, one of which is just visible.

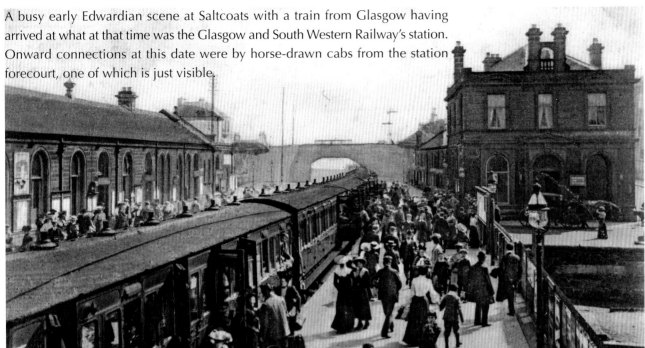

Countess Street, Saltcoats

Left: At the same location around 1922, a wagonette awaits custom. SD 3375 was a GMC with open sides and fold-down canvas side screens which would be used according to weather conditions. It was owned by Dugald McGregor of Saltcoats who was later a member of the Clyde Coast Services partnership. The sign in the front window reads 'Ardrossan & Saltcoats 3d'.

Opposite: The main Saltcoats bus stance at the top of Countess Street was conveniently opposite the railway station. This mid-1920s scene shows a variety of vehicles assembled for business, which was largely the short shuttle along to Ardrossan. The front row shows Ford SD 1597, GMC SD 9415 and Guy SD 3944.

Although Dunoon lies only a twenty minute sail across the Firth from Gourock, the Cowal Peninsula is a marvellous other world to those who appreciate scenery and space to enjoy its many wonders of nature. The fact that even today the attractions of Cowal are underestimated helps keep the area all the more appealing to its afficionados. In many ways transport connections to, from and within the peninsula are better than ever, so a day excursion from the Glasgow area is simple. Walkers, for instance, on a morning ferry can catch West Coast Motors' bus to Carrick Castle, a splendid run via the shores of Lock Eck, Hell's Glen and Lochgoilhead. From Carrick an easy walk by forestry tracks leads to Ardentinny where an hourly service brings you back to Dunoon. This single example is one of simply so many – Puck's Glen, Benmore Botanic Gardens, Glenbranter, Toward and walk back (again via the scenic forestry tracks found throughout the peninsula) to Innellan and return by bus. Or why not enjoy a whole day of splendid scenery and use the Dunoon to Rothesay bus via the Colintraive Ferry and return home by the Wemyss Bay boat and connecting rail to Glasgow? Longer but still an easy option is the West Coast bus from Dunoon to Tighnabruaich and Portavadie thence ferry across Loch Fyne to Tarbert and bus home.

From Victorian times when many city businessmen chose to build a villa on the Cowal shore, Dunoon became an increasingly popular place for excursionists, either for a day's sail 'Doon the Watter' or for a lengthier stay if funds and time permitted. There was always a wide range of tours available, originally by horse-drawn coach and this added to the town's attractions. The stance for such delights was always as adjacent as possible to the pierhead where representatives of the various competing companies were quick to point out the superiority of their tour. Looking towards the Argyll Hotel in the early 1920s we see the tour stance at that time, with a selection of waiting charabancs loading for business. There would appear to be no shortage of prospective customers on this occasion. The charabancs visible are Commers owned by Ernest Hartley who really pioneered the tourist trade where the new motor vehicles gradually usurped the horse-drawn coaches. By getting in on the ground floor in Dunoon, Hartley was able to build up a good business before the many others who followed.

By the late 1930s, the town stance had become considerably busier with the coaches of rival Dunoon firms, principally Antonelli, Baird and Fitzpatrick, vying for custom. This view (with several extra pedestrians drawn in by the postcard company artist to make the scene appear even busier) shows a typical summer scene. Not only is there a selection of locally based Bedford, Chevrolet, Dodge and Leyland vehicles, owned by Charles Fitzpatrick's Silver Line (who acquired Hartley's business – the light coloured coaches to the left) and Alexander Baird's Blue Line (the four to the right) but also four Central SMT Leyland Tigers on a day excursion from Lanarkshire are parked at the old coal pier. Also visible is an Albion of Dunoon Motor Services on a local service to Sandbank. Note that every single coach had either a fully fold-back canvas hood or a 'sunshine' type roof, all open on what must have been a mild summer day.

The 'far-famed' Lock Eck Tour was one of the most popular excursions available, originally combining a variety of superb Highland scenery with different modes of travel, making for a delightful day out. City folks could come down by train from St. Enoch at 8.05 a.m. to Greenock (Princes Pier) for a departure at 8.50 a.m. or from Central at 8.20 a.m. connecting with the 9.13 a.m. sailing from Gourock, thence by *Queen Alexandra* or, from 1927, by *King George V* across to Dunoon where one could make a choice: either remain on board for the sail via Rothesay, the Kyles of Bute and Tighnabruaich and thence to Inveraray, returning by charabanc to Dunoon or alternatively, the other way round, disembarking at Dunoon to join Baird's motor coach for Loch Eck and Inveraray, and returning by steamer.

When this view of the Loch Eck tour coaches leaving Strachur was captured in 1906, they were horse-drawn and the imposing driver always wore a grey top hat contrasting with his scarlet tunic. These Edwardian days perhaps saw the tour at its best, especially for variety. Setting off from Dunoon anti-clockwise by horse coach via Sandbank to Inverchapel at the southern end of Loch Eck, passengers would then join the steamer *Fairy Queen*, built by Seath of Rutherglen in 1878, for the cruise to the top end of the loch, where coaches would continue to Strachur to join the Inveraray sailing. After around an hour here the return journey was made by steamer via Loch Fyne, Tighnabruaich, Kyles of Bute, Rothesay and so home to Dunoon. The tour could also be enjoyed in the opposite direction. After *Fairy Queen*'s final season in 1926, the tour was necessarily amended to use motor coaches (owned by Alex Baird of Dunoon) which operated all the way to Inveraray to join the steamer returning with those passengers who had opted to take the tour clockwise. The only current reminder of those halcyon days are a few rotting timber beams on the Inverchapel shore which have survived as parts of the old pier.

An early description of *Fairy Queen*, seen here at Inverchapel Pier at the south end of Loch Eck in late Victorian times, detailed her as "a neat little screw vessel, 70 feet long by 12 at the beam with a raised deck 40 feet in length covering a small saloon which opens gondola fashion to the front for ladies and another towards the stern for a smoking room. Both of these handsome little bowers are well-ventilated all round and fitted up with lavatories etc. The certificate authorises 150 passengers".

The Loch Eck Tour originated around 1828 when David Napier, the Clyde steam pioneer (who had built the boiler for the first *Comet*) constructed a pier, hotel and villas at Kilmun on the Holy Loch, from where he built a new road to Loch Eck. Napier was a shrewd entrepreneur and in order to benefit and boost his own interests, was responsible for the first road transport connections in the Clyde Coast area. He ran steamers between the Broomielaw and Kilmun, where passengers boarded a steam coach (also built by Napier) for Inverchapel on Loch Eck. There they connected with the little *Aglaia*, the first passenger steamer to be built of iron, and sailed the full length of the loch to connect with another steam coach for Strachur from where they sailed the remaining few miles across Loch Fyne to Inveraray. Horse-drawn coaches later displaced the steam coach and sailings on the loch were in time revived by *Fairy Queen*, but basically Napier's tour remained the same for approximately a century.

An atmospheric Edwardian glimpse of the Clachan, Strachur, as the horse-drawn coach tackles the steep Clachan Brae on its way to join the steamer at the head of Loch Eck on the return leg of the tour. Not by choice, but on the order of the coachman, male passengers with their headgear of straw boaters pant up the brae on foot through the haze of dust cast up by the toiling coach and horses. The ladies, however, were allowed to remain on board. One of the new breed of automobiles in the shape of a little two seat cycle car sits across from Montgomery's smiddy. Far-sighted Willie Montgomery was not just a blacksmith, but also a pioneer motor dealer in the area; he held the first Ford agency in Argyllshire and later ran the service bus between Strachur and Dunoon.

The 'far-famed' Loch Eck Tour has arrived at Inveraray around 1902 with what appears to be a capacity crowd on board *Lord of the Isles*, a magnificent steamer built in 1891 by D and W Henderson to replace the 1877 original of the same name for the Glasgow & Inveraray Steamboat Company and often described as a "floating palace". An open charabanc with bench seats awaits customers – and just look at that delightful pram leading the line down the pier. To the left is *Fairy*, the diminutive ferry across Loch Fyne to St. Catherine's.

Friction on Loch Fyne. The launch in 1901, at Denny's of Dumbarton, of the world's first commercial turbine steamer introduced a new era to Clyde Coast shipping. *King Edward* was operated by Captain John Williamson initially between Greenock, Dunoon, Rothesay, Fairlie, Lochranza and Campbeltown but by 1903 was sailing via the south end of Bute all the way to Inveraray. From 1909 she sailed instead via the Kyles of Bute, competing directly with *Lord of the Isles*. There was no contest really, with the superior speed of the turbine allowing *King Edward* to berth first and, moreover, simply stay put, adding to the chagrin of those on board the '*Lord*'. Encapsulating the situation, here we see *King Edward* at Inveraray while a frustrated *Lord of the Isles* frets offshore.

Left: The cover of the official guide booklet for the Loch Eck Tour issued by the Lochgoil and Inveraray Steamboat Company for several years featured this colourful scene on an open charabanc featuring a typical coachman of the period, traditionally garbed in scarlet tunic and silver top hat.

OFFICIAL GUIDE

LOCHGOIL AND INVERARAY STEAMBOAT COY.'S

FAR-FAMED

LOCH ECK TOUR

ESTABLISHED 1878

SIR THOMAS KELLY, C.A., Secretary, 34 West George Street, Glasgow.

Below: In the days when the 'far-famed' Loch Eck Tour combined sailing on *Fairy Queen* with travel by horse-drawn coach, these coaches would provide the link between Dunoon and Inverchapel, at the southern end of Loch Eck, and from the north end of the loch to Strachur to join the Inveraray steamer. Here we see a well-patronised *Queen Alexandra* of 1912 at Strachur Pier which closed, never to re-open, in 1935.

Another vessel built by Denny was *King George V*, commissioned in 1926, year of the General Strike. Her attractive lines are seen to advantage in the black-hulled livery of Turbine Steamers Ltd., with black-topped white funnels at Inveraray around 1930, prior to transfer to the MacBrayne fleet in 1935. This view was taken from the appropriately named waterfront buildings known as 'Ferryland'.

King George V sweeps towards Tighnabruaich Pier in the 1927 season, when only a year old. This scene, looking past Ardlamont Point and over to the Arran Hills also shows the village of Kames, upper right. It was titled 'West Kyles of Bute' by local photographer Cuthbert Spencer of Tighnabruaich who produced a series of picture postcards of the area in the 1920s and 30s.

Loch Eck Tour, Cars and Steamer at Inveraray CS 701

Captain Williamson's fast turbine *Queen Alexandra* of 1902 became the natural consort of *King Edward*, but had a relatively short life, ending in flames at Greenock's Albert Harbour in 1911. Denny's then built a replacement *Queen Alexandra* which appeared the following season. By the time she was withdrawn (as *Saint Columba*) in September 1958 she was the oldest Clyde steamer by an easy margin of almost twenty years. Here she is at Inveraray around 1927, connections provided by Vulcan charabancs in the fleet of Baird of Dunoon waiting to depart by road with passengers on the 'far-famed' Loch Eck Tour. The private hire car on the right is a left-hand-drive example of the famous 'Tin Lizzie' or Model T Ford.

SILVER LINE
Famed

LOCH ECK TOUR

CIRCULAR TOUR BY LAND AND SEA

Motor Coach-De-Luxe leaves Dunoon on Mondays;
Wednesdays, Thursdays and Fridays,

at 10-30 a.m.
FOR

INVERARAY

Via Holy Loch, Benmore, Loch Eck, Glenbranter,
Strachur, Loch Fyne, St. Catherines, Cairndow and
Loch Shira.

PASSENGERS RETURN BY STEAMER
AT 2-20 P.M.
FOR

DUNOON

Via Loch Fyne, and the Famous Kyles of Bute.

FARE FOR THE ROUND - 7/3

Passengers desirous of travelling Saloon on Steamer
may do so at an additional charge.

BE CAREFUL TO BOOK IN ADVANCE WITH
SILVER LINE AGENTS, OR AT THE

Silver Line Booking Office
PAVILION BUILDINGS,
DUNOON.

Phone 26.   Phone 26.

WILLSONS', LE'STER.

A decade later the Lock Eck Tour continued to be just as popular. The vessel on this occasion (around 1937) at Inveraray is *Duchess of Montrose* built by Denny of Dumbarton to the order of the LMS Railway, first seeing service in the 1930 season. In the foreground an open Albion charabanc awaits trade.

ST. CATHERINE'S HOTEL, LOCH FYNE.   21/579. J.V.

Watering holes on the tour were all-important for those participating in the motor coach leg of the journey which originated with the withdrawal of *Fairy Queen* on Loch Eck in 1926. From this time the tour involved a drive by motor coach all the way to Inveraray. Facilities for refreshments which were available on board the steamers were of course not possible on a charabanc. Perhaps most popular for a natural break to provide the necessary comforts around halfway on the journey was St. Catherine's Hotel. During just such a break in the 1931 season we see three charabancs in the Dunoon based fleet of Alexander Baird who operated under the 'Royal Blue Line' title. Prominent in front are two Vulcans, built in Southport by a company which supplied 25 double deckers to Glasgow Corporation in the early 1930s. SB 2590 of 1925 has its hood folded right back to allow passengers to enjoy the summer sunshine. Newer SB 3588 was a Vulcan Duchess model of 1930.

In earlier years St. Catherine's had been the base for the mail run via the wild Hell's Glen to Lochgoilhead, connecting there with the steamer to and from Greenock. Travel initially was by horse-drawn coach but eventually was superseded by a motor wagonette. Both were operated by Alan MacDonald, proprietor of St. Catherine's Hotel. The upper scene shows the laden horse-drawn mail coach *en route* from Lochgoilhead in the early 1900s at Moses' Well in Hell's Glen (where you can still to this day enjoy spring water from the lion's mouth). Presumably the coachman has allowed the horses a rest before continuing the long climb to the summit and then the steep descent to Loch Fyne.

Model T Ford SB 1357 was purchased in 1921 with 12 seat wagonette bodywork built by Mitchell of Greenock. It is seen at St. Catherine's in 1924 with James Macdonald, the owner's son, on the right and his cousin, Willie MacRae, who acted as 'conductor'. In 1926, due to a re-organisation of the mails, their contract ended. In the 1850s, this had been the preferred route of travel for Glasgow author Hugh MacDonald, best known for *Rambles Round Glasgow*. In his companion volume *Days at the Coast* MacDonald describes his journey to Inveraray via Lochgoilhead, Hell's Glen and ferry from St. Catherine's. It's a recommended read for anyone interested in travel as it once was.

The salvation of Hunter's Quay Pier lay with its survival into the era of Western Ferries' shuttle car ferries. This was how the old pier looked around 1900 with *Galatea* calling on the Caledonian Steam Packet's run to Gourock. She was relatively short-lived, sailing only between 1889 and 1906. Hunter's Quay was named after James Hunter of Hafton, local landowner and speculator.

Almost next door was Kirn Pier, only half a mile from Hunter's Quay towards Dunoon, but which closed for sailings at the end of 1963. The year of this view is 1949, when various steamers still visited regularly. Here the Denny-built turbine steamer *Duchess of Argyll* calls *en route* for Dunoon and Rothesay. By this time she was a grand old lady, having entered Caley service in 1906 and was amongst the fastest of the Clyde steamers. Meanwhile the puffer *Cuban* unloads to a waiting wagon.

Apart from the busy tour operations based in Dunoon, local connections by bus on the Cowal Peninsula were provided in pre-war years by a number of small firms, some on a route unique to themselves and others sharing the busier, more lucrative runs such as north to Sandbank or south to Innellan and Toward. Prior to the Road Traffic Act of 1930 when order was brought to bus operations, things were largely a free-for-all. Local town councils such as that in Dunoon often demanded an annual fee for the use of a stance, for which a so-called 'licence' was issued, but largely these were a simple means to obtain extra revenue. Some burghs also licensed drivers and conductors. Typical of the smaller operators was Daniel McFarlane's ABC (Argyll Bus Co.) based at the Argyll Garage, Alexandra Parade, which commenced running to Sandbank via the shore road and to Toward in April 1928 with SB 3093, a new purchase on the then popular American-built Reo chassis. Although making a minor impact initially, ABC survived only until the early 1930s.

Dunoon area bus operators working local runs were numerous in the late 1920s and early 1930s and included Michael Antonelli (Primrose Garage), T.S. Blackham (Benmore Motor Services), Brown's Bus Service (to Glen Lean), Bell's Red Line, McDiarmid of Innellan, and Charles Fitzpatrick. Competition was intense and survival was only possible for the fittest. Dunoon Motor Services (Sam Crawford and William Hill) built up a reliable local network and developed a new fleet of mainly Albion buses, including the 20 seater Victor seen here. It hurries along Alexandra Parade on a quiet summer Sunday morning in 1936 to connect with *Jeanie Deans*, already berthed at the pier.

Queen Mary II disembarks at Dunoon in the summer of 1948, with the hands of the pier clock at 12.15, while operating the classic 'Doon the Watter' cruise from Bridge Wharf to the Arran Coast. Spectators, no doubt with Scottish country dance music in their ears, lean over the old pier balcony watching the incoming visitors. This was an obligatory occasion in any Dunoon holiday, but now no longer an option as the balcony area was demolished in 1982.

On the same day in 1948 at Dunoon, the Caledonian Steam Packet's *Marchioness of Lorne* pauses to pick up passengers on her stately round of the Holy Loch piers, never having a reputation for being the speediest. Built at Fairfield's in 1935, she lay quite low in the water and was also recognisable by her low bridge and lack of observation deck over the deckhouses. Until her withdrawal in 1954 the '*Marchioness*' spent most of her time on the Blairmore – Strone – Kilmun – Hunter's Quay – Kirn – Dunoon circuit.

Jeanie Deans pays a visit to Dunoon in the early 1960s, captured by the camera in this fine bows-on shot, probably *en route* from Craigendoran to Rothesay. The community of Kirn may be seen across the bay, where a pier existed at the point until the 1990s. It saw its final steamer departure in December 1963.

Baird's Motor Tours.

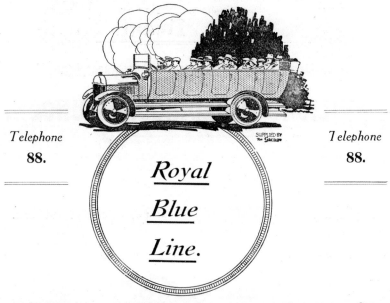

Telephone **88.**

Telephone **88.**

Royal

Blue

Line.

SUPPLIED BY The Garage

The Cars with the reputation for comfort.

SPECIAL DAILY TOURS.

St. Catherine's, Ardentinny, Loch Eck, Whistlefield, Glen-masson, etc.

SPECIAL ONE DAY TOURS.

INVERARAY.

Splendid 80 Miles Tour, via Loch Eck, Glenbranter Estate, Strachur, and Round the Shore of Loch Fyne to the Capital of Argyll.

CIRCULAR TOUR, THE SEVEN LOCHS.

Via Loch Eck, Loch Fyne, Rest-and-be-Thankful, Loch Long, Arrochar, Loch Lomond, Crianlarich, Tyndrum, Dalmally, Loch Awe, Inveraray, etc.

OBAN.

165 Miles Tour through Magnificent Scenery, via Loch Eck, Loch Fyne, Inveraray, Glen Aray, Dalmally, Loch Awe, through the Pass of Brander, to Oban.

All kinds of Motor Cars and Horse Carriages for hire.

OUR CARS CAN BE BOOKED FOR PRIVATE PARTIES TO GO ANYWHERE.

BOOKING OFFICES: PAVILION BUILDINGS, Pier Rd., Jane St. & Argyll St., Dunoon.

BAIRD'S OF DUNOON

LUXURY COACHES

DAY & AFTERNOON TOURS FROM DUNOON

Baird's of Dunoon

WEST END GARAGE AUCHAMORE ROAD DUNOON

Tel. Dunoon 2088

Booking Office

Argyll Gardens

Tel. Dunoon 2438

for **WESTERN HIGHLANDS COACH TOURING**

Special Quotations for Private Parties

Phone **Dunoon 2088**★

FOR

BAIRD'S RADIO TAXIS

Opposite page: Contrast in coach advertising 1920s and 1960s. Alexander Baird was one of the pioneering Dunoon coaching companies which started in Victorian times with horse-drawn charabancs meeting steamers at the pier to take passengers on a variety of scenic local excursions. Baird was later than rival Ernest Hartley to introduce motor tours, thus losing out a little. By the early 1920s, however, he realised that survival meant change and started to replace his horse-drawn vehicles with motor equivalents, although as we see from the 1925 advert, equine options were still available at this time. Although admittedly nostalgic, I find the early ad so much more satisfying to my eyes than the characterless later one. The drawings, incidentally, are based on one of Baird's 1920s Vulcan charabancs and a 1960s Bedford.

Hunter's Quay Pier as it is today, with the recent completion of a new linkspan, looking over the mouth of Holy Loch towards Strone Point. Western Ferries' 2001 vessel *Sound of Scarba* built at Ferguson's yard in Port Glasgow (as was the linkspan) delivers the Dunoon-bound 'City Connect' bus operated by McGill's of Greenock. This service operates several times daily from Glasgow via Braehead Shopping Centre to Cowal and incorporates the Western Ferries' sailings to and from McInroy's Point, thus obviating the need for change of transport. On this occasion in August 2009 the vehicle was Volvo/Jonckheere Y376 BFS.

Local services also link at Hunter's Quay. Dennis Dart DK05 FWB works West Coast Motors' Dunoon area town service between the Hunter's Quay Holiday Village, Upper Kirn and Dunoon town centre. West Coast's service between Dunoon, Sandbank and Ardentinny also passes Western Ferries' terminal for sailings to the Inverclyde shore. The 1963-built *Sound of Sanda*, seen loading at the linkspan, came to Cowal in 1996 from Amsterdam and was converted at the Garvel yard in Greenock.

In the early 1960s services on the Cowal Peninsula were largely operated with a fleet of secondhand double deckers by Dunoon Motor Services. Two are seen here, having just squeezed past on a narrow section of the shore road at Hunter's Quay. Bound for Benmore via Puck's Glen is CCK 635, an all-Leyland PD2 of 1948 which had originally served with Ribble Motor Services, while heading to Dunoon is a former Bury Corporation Leyland PD1.

Again typical of early 1960s Dunoon, we see three DMS double deckers in their red and cream livery at the pierhead stance. Leyland Titan PD1 EN 8538 with Roe bodywork started life with Bury Corporation in 1946 and will leave for Sandbank via the High Road. Two Albion Venturers follow, former Western SMT (originally Young of Paisley) XS 4774 of 1938 with ECW re-body is serving upper Hunter's Quay while Roberts-bodied FYS 270 came from Glasgow Corporation and is on the longer service to Ardentinny on Long Long, via the Holy Loch villages of Sandbank, Kilmun and Strone. To the left, DSB 126 is a Duple-bodied Bedford 'SB' coach in the Gold Line fleet.

Cowal Games, held over the last weekend of August, is always the busiest time of the year in Dunoon. Bus enthusiasts have a field day, with visiting vehicles from near and far. This late 1950s scene at the entry to the Games' Field shows a line up of pipe band coaches, headed by elderly Dunoon Motor Services' Leyland Tiger/Duple RN 7745, a former Ribble coach of 1936 working the shuttle service to and from town for Games' spectators. Bus and steamer proprietors all benefit from a hectic time operationally, with many extra services provided by both.

Rock Cafe 1930s. Cowal Games Saturday 2008. Heavy police presence at the pier but nothing more sinister than crowd control. West Coast Motors' Volvo P200 WCM leaves for Inveraray, while behind and specially drafted in for the day is a Dennis Dart of sister company Glasgow Citybus, working the town local service. Setting the scene quite nicely is *Waverley*, paddling away in a broad arc from the new pier, which still awaits use by CalMac.

P.S. *Waverley* always presents a pretty picture. Her paddles reverse to disturb the otherwise calm waters of Loch Long in August 2009 as she negotiates alongside the rebuilt pier at Blairmore *en route* to Lochgoilhead on a Wednesdays only sailing. The fine weather has encouraged a good number of local folk to board here and enjoy the short cruise, some of whom have arrived on a chartered West Coast Motors' former Lothian Region Volvo Olympian. The Ardentinny – Dunoon service also provides a connection at Blairmore, where the attractive pier closed between 1997 and 2005 for refurbishment which will hopefully bring further future business.

The link between Dunoon/Rothesay and Portavadie, providing connection on the CalMac ferry across Loch Fyne to Tarbert, was served for some years by Forrester of Portavadie (Wee Geoff's Buses) but with Geoff's retiral in 2009 the work is now handled by West Coast Motors. This view at Portavadie on an autumn evening in 2005 shows W33 GEF, Geoff's appropriately registered Autobus-bodied Mercedes-Benz 31 seater, which was his final bus.

Same location at Portavadie but after West Coast Motors had assumed control. On this occasion their connecting bus with the Tarbert ferry was SF54 HWA, a Plaxton Beaver-bodied Mercedes Vario.

Across Loch Fyne at Tarbert certain sailings are met by a West Coast Motors connection to Skipness. Seen awaiting a mid-afternoon arrival of CalMac's *Isle of Cumbrae* in August 2006 is HC04 CHS, a KVC-bodied Mercedes which West Coast Motors acquired from Henderson Hiring of Tarbert, the previous operator of the service.

West Coast Motors have had a presence in Tarbert, Loch Fyne since commencing their Campbeltown – Tarbert service in 1922. With their acquisition in 1949 of the shuttle service between the boats formerly operated by the motor section of Dickie Bros. the boatbuilders, West Coast Motors inherited the bus link between the steamer from Gourock at the East Loch and the Islay vessel at Tarbert's West Loch Pier. Burlingham-bodied Leyland Tiger SB 8080, new in 1950, has loaded up from *Lochnevis* at the East Loch Pier with Islay-bound passengers in summer 1966.

In the mid-1960s also at the East Pier, traffic justified two buses, with Bedford SB/Duple GSB 571 and Bedford/Duple Bella Vista CDC 496C both in attendance, as passengers disembark from MacBrayne's recently arrived *Lochfyne*.

Right: From the earliest days of the motorbus there was competition with the Gareloch steamer as Watt's Gareloch Motor Service Co. of Helensburgh was one of Scotland's pioneering bus companies. This company started operations in the early 1900s between Helensburgh, Garelochhead and Clynder, where a bus was stationed overnight, working into Helensburgh early in the morning to connect with the Glasgow train. Outside company headquarters in Helensburgh at the granary, West Clyde Street around 1906 is the fleet comprising what to modern eyes appear extremely primitive open vehicles, but which in fact were cutting edge at the time. Wagonettes SN 150 and 136 were both Wolseleys while G 724 and SN 185 were Albions, as was hire car SY 51.

By the 1920s, Henry Brown and Co. of Garelochhead operated the bus services around the Gareloch. One of his most unusual buses was DGO 500, the unique former London Transport six wheel AEC Q, seen here with mechanics in attendance outside the garage in 1949. Interestingly the destination screen shows Gully Ferry as an intermediate point *en route* although it had not operated across the Gareloch for many years. Garelochhead Pier had closed on outbreak of war in 1939 to be followed during the war by the remaining lochside ports of call. In 1951 John Foy took over from Henry Brown until the business closed in 1980. Since then the Gareloch has been served by a number of different operators.

Perhaps the most popular Clyde steamer with the public was the one which survived longer than any other, in fact the last of the Victorian Clyde paddlers. *Lucy Ashton* was built at Seath's of Rutherglen in 1888 and continued to see service until 1949 by which time she had attained 61 years, celebrating her diamond jubilee in 1948. For most of her life she was based at Craigendoran (initially with the North British Railway fleet) and sailed the Gareloch circuit calling at Helensburgh and the small lochside piers at Rosneath and Clynder. This view shows 'Lucy' at Garelochhead in 1934 as part of the LNER fleet with the famous funnel colours of red with black top, divided by a white band. She is about to depart on the final sailing of the day, working back at 5.35 p.m. to Craigendoran where she will connect with trains to Dumbarton and Glasgow. The Gareloch service was an early casualty to bus competition, in this instance services provided by Brown of Garelochhead with connections from there to Kilcreggan and Coulport. Steamer sailings on the Gareloch largely ceased during wartime and were not continued at the end of hostilities.

Right: Commercial connections were provided on Clydeside by a variety of haulage contractors who could often transport goods at cheaper rates than the competing steamer companies, who often did not have much available space for such items in any case. An example was the Clyde and Campbeltown Shipping Co. which supplemented rather than competed with their own vessels sailing to Ardrishaig, Tarbert and Campbeltown in particular. Amongst their fleet of mainly Albion lorries was GG 4074, a model 473 four-tonner of 1931 and seen here in 1938 rounding the top hairpin bend on the old 'Rest and Be Thankful' road to Argyllshire. Only short wheelbase vehicles with a good steering lock could negotiate this top bend in one attempt.

Above: Several of the Argyllshire carriers' quarters in the city were conveniently in the dockside Broomielaw area. For instance, Argyll Transports of Lochgilphead, owned by George Thom and Alex Matheson, had a Glasgow base in James Watt Street, where two of their 1933 Albion three-ton lorries are loading. Both carry Greenock licence numbers, VS 2399 and 2422 respectively, as they were built and registered there by coachbuilders and Albion dealers J. Mitchell & Sons. Livery was an attractive light grey with a red band and chassis.

Also built and registered in Greenock by Mitchell the coachbuilder was VS 2872, a similar model 473 Albion to the others, but owned by Cowal haulier William Mitchell (no connection). Its headboard announces a daily service between Glasgow and Strone, where Mitchell's premises at Tyneshandon were adjacent to the pier.

Portincaple's main claim to fame for many years was perhaps the unusual home of local inhabitant and 'character' Susie McGlone. Known as 'Susie's Castle', it was captured on postcards by several publishers, particularly in the Edwardian era when folk travelled for quite a distance to view this curiosity. The 'castle' was in fact an upturned fishing smack. It had formerly been owned by the McNab family of Ferry House who derived an income from fishing and also provided the ferry service across Loch Long. This early 1900s scene shows Susie, complete with clay pipe and cats.

Even after the withdrawal of the 'push-and-pull' steam train in November 1959 between Arrochar and Tarbet Station and Craigendoran, a connection was maintained by British Railways over the route by means of this railbus. That period saw this type of vehicle replace several Scottish steam operations in an attempt to avoid line closures and still save revenue.

A classic connection at Arrochar and Tarbet Station where the train has just arrived from Glasgow to be met by the bus for Lochgoilhead which at that time was operated by Noble of Clydebank, trading under the name Weir's Tours. Perhaps a Saturday sale was on in the city judging by these heavily-laden ladies. Noble's bus was Talbot Pullman triaxle G213 AHP, used on the route from 1992 till 1995.

One of the many long-forgotten ferries was that at Portincaple from where a small boat sailed across Loch Long to Mark. This view from the shore looks over the loch to its isolated Ardgartan forest side on a dull day in 1952 when *Marchioness of Graham* was performing an excursion from Ayr to Arrochar. She sends out a significant bow wave as she speeds down the loch and the wee boys in the rowing boat will soon feel the force of the waves reaching the shore.

Arrochar at the turn of the century, with the North British Railway paddler *Lady Rowena* in attendance. The short connecting journey across the isthmus to Tarbet was made by the waiting horse-drawn coaches, which would convey the passengers to join a steamer on Loch Lomond to continue their circular tour. Each of the children is wearing a hat even in those far-off days.

From Craigendoran in the 1950s and 60s, indeed until 1972, there was still the option to sail via Dunoon, Blairmore and Lochgoilhead to Arrochar. These sailings were latterly operated by *Waverley*, but on Saturdays a 'Maid' class vessel was often found on the run. *Maid of Cumbrae* is seen at Arrochar in 1965, while the inset shows one of her sisters, *Maid of Skelmorlie*. That year she also made the final call at Lochgoilhead, but is seen at Arrochar with MSN 195, a Trojan minibus of MacTavish of Arrochar, operator of the short link service between Arrochar and Tarbet on Loch Lomond.

Above: When MacBraynes withdrew their Lochgoilhead sailings in 1946 the company substituted their own replacement bus service, linking Carrick Castle with Lochgoilhead and teminating at Arrochar and Tarbet Station where onward connections by train were available to Glasgow. In the 1960s this route was sensibly cut back as a cost-cutting exercise to end at the isolated Lochgoilhead road end at the summit of the 'Rest and Be Thankful' hill road. There the bus from 'the Goil' would connect with MacBraynes main road buses to Glasgow and to Loch Fyneside. This scene at 'Top of Rest', with Loch Restil in the background, shows the morning link between the bus (on this occasion duplicated) from Glasgow to Tarbert, Loch Fyne, and the Carrick Castle connection. As well as passengers, mails and parcels were also transferred between the buses which on this occasion in April 1969 were EGA 834C (146), the regular Lochgoilhead-based Bedford VAS/Duple Midland 29 seater of 1965, and 198 CUS (63), an AEC Reliance/Duple Midland 41 seater of 1961. The front bus, also an AEC Reliance, is AGE 545B (194), a 1964 model with Duple 43 seat body.

Overleaf: Carrick Castle lay at the other end of the scenic route. When I took this shot on an autumn afternoon in 1962, I was employed as a conductor by MacBrayne at their Glasgow depot in Parliamentary Road and often took advantage of a day off to explore parts of Argyll then unknown to me. At this time these little Bedfords were approaching their demise and quite a few had already been withdrawn from other parts of MacBrayne's extensive bus world. They were favourites of mine being so traditional and one only has to judge the style of replacement seen above to agree that in comparison the later vehicle totally lacked the character and individuality of the 1950s model. Indeed I recall the MacBrayne crews referring to the arrival of the new box-like Bedfords as being akin to breadvans. Bedford KGD 906 (165) dated from 1952 and had a Duple Sportsman style of body. In earlier years steamers called at Carrick Pier beside the castle *en route* from Lochgoilhead to Gourock, but the final year for this sailing was 1946.

Blairlodge School,
Polmont Stn
22 nd March 190?

D.E.

"Whit wey
hae ye no
written tae
me? Hae ye
taken the sulks

"WEE MACGREEGOR."

yours. D.J.

Above: Rothesay, perhaps even more so than Dunoon, is redolent of memories of days 'Doon the Watter' for countless Glasgow folk. Rothesay, remember, was where Glasgow's inimitable Edwardian scamp 'Wee MacGreegor' came to holiday with maw, paw and gran'paw. Rothesay, of course, like Glasgow, had trams, which subconsciously perhaps created a further bond between Brandanes and Glaswegians. This postcard was sent in 1903 from Polmont to Leith and features J.J. Bell's mischief making 'Wee MacGreegor'.

0805 GUILDFORD SQUARE, ROTHESAY. Poulton.

Victorian Rothesay, looking from Guildford Square along the harbour side towards Craigmore. The vessel at the pier is an early Caledonian steamer while prominent is one of the Tramways Co. horse cars. Rothesay Tramways opened for business between the pierhead at Guildford Square and Port Bannatyne in 1882, with twelve single deck horse cars. Seen above is No. 6, one of the original canopied cross bench cars built in Sheffield with eight transverse rows of seats. Later similar cars were built locally by Malcolm's boatyard and others by Lander of Rothesay. In 1902 new electric trams with open bodies and cross bench seating replaced the horse cars.

ETTRICK BAY

DEPOT

An extension of the route from Port Bannatyne in 1905 took the trams over to the sands of Ettrick Bay on the east side of Bute. This wonderfully atmospheric view taken in July 1928 at Ettrick Bay shows the arrival of No. 12, a completely open 'toastrack' type of tram which was one of two constructed in 1919 by Mitchell of Greenock in the tramway depot at Pointhouse, Ardbeg, which today is the local bus depot occupied by West Coast Motors. The run across the island must have been an exhilarating experience on a toastrack, no doubt spiced further by the genial repartee of a full load of (mainly) Glaswegians. Schoolboys and girls with their parents prepare to scramble aboard as soon as the car stops and the incoming passengers clamber down from their perches on the wooden bench seats. Already the teenage conductor in white-topped uniform cap has jumped down from the slowing tram to swing the trolley pole around preparatory to an on-time trip back to town. The tramways company advert posted prominently on the front dash of No. 12 reads "the finest drive in Bute by Electric Tramcar right across the island to Ettrick Bay". This was the heyday of Bute's tramway, when Rothesay was regarded by many as the only holiday destination. However, by 1931 the operation had become seasonal and after the summer of 1936 the trams were totally replaced by buses, thus ending over half a century of rails from Rothesay.

On arrival at Ettrick Bay, even on a dull day when the sun did not shine, there was always plenty to occupy the time of youngsters and oldsters alike. Aeroplane flights and stunts, sand castle competitions, donkey rides, even goats pulled buggies with small children along the sands! Refreshments of course were available at the soda fountain but the main attraction was the Pavilion. Both were owned by the tramways company. There was, however, yet another delight for boys big and small, a real steam-powered miniature railway. The 15" gauge track ran in a big circle next to the Pavilion and the coal-burning locomotive named *Samson* was owned personally by John C. Sword, aviation pioneer, vintage car collector and general manager of Western SMT, the parent company of Rothesay Tramways. *Samson* was an American built Cagney 4-4-0 dating from about 1903 which Sword had later acquired as an avid collector and the railway was in place at Ettrick Bay for the summer season of 1936, the last season of the trams. It closed in early wartime but opened at Millport for a couple of seasons after the war.

From 1937 and during all seasons which followed the end of the tramway system in 1936, the mainstay of the Rothesay – Ettrick Bay bus route was a fleet of secondhand former Western SMT (and originally Scottish Transport) Tilling Stevens of 1931 vintage with new completely open-sided and unglazed bodywork by Burlingham of Blackpool, specially built to resemble the open trams. A typical example of the 'blue buses', as they were then known, loads at Ettrick Bay in 1938.

Throughout the 1920s and early 1930s there was much competition amongst a number of bus companies running in opposition to the Rothesay trams, the largest of which was McKirdy and McMillan of Rothesay with over twenty buses. The tramways company had inaugurated its own buses in 1925 to help counteract competition and as time progressed acquired the businesses of most of the remaining rivals, including McKellar of Craigmore, Brennan of Craigmore, Bell of Rothesay, McGarrity of Rothesay and McKirdy and McMillan. One of the small firms acquired was Martin Bros. of Rothesay in 1936. Here we see Bryce Martin with his schoolboy conductor in the late 1920s and SJ 527, his claret-coloured Morris charabanc on a competing journey with the trams at Ettrick Bay.

One local company which did not sell out until the 1950s was Yeates' Rothesay Motor Services which operated the scenic route over the Canada Hill viewpoint. When this firm finished in 1955 it was acquired not by Western SMT, which then held the island monopoly, but surprisingly by McGill's Bus Service of Barrhead. This mid-1960s view at the pierhead shows KYB 8, a Duple-bodied Bedford OB of Rothesay Motor Services (McGill retained the name) alongside JSD 911 (RT 1275) one of several of this type of Bristol, bodied by Alexander and based at Pointhouse for the Bute operations of Western SMT.

Shhh... one almost feels like tiptoeing past the slumbering paddler *Queen-Empress* berthed overnight at Kilchattan Bay. She lay here preparatory to her early sailing at 6.45 a.m. for Millport, Keppel, Fairlie, Largs and Wemyss Bay, conveying the morning commuters to work on the mainland. Built in 1912 by Murdoch & Murray of Port Glasgow she initially served with the Williamson fleet before becoming a troopship and minesweeper during the 1914-18 hostilities. This atmospheric view dates from 1938, by which year she bore the buff and black-topped funnel of the LMS fleet. After again serving as a minesweeper during the Second World War she was sold for breaking up.

The southern extremity of regular bus operations on Bute has always been the village of Kilchattan Bay. This 1938 scene shows (with good eyesight) an Albion single decker, which passed from the acquired McKirdy and McMillan fleet to Rothesay Tramways in 1936, arriving from Rothesay. Playing on the pier are two children who are very much a reminder of that era and indeed the post-war period also. They are no doubt enjoying this island holiday but the boy still wears his school blazer and grey shorts, along with the obligatory summer sandals and ankle socks, while the wee lassie sports a kilt and classic Fair Isle cardigan. *Morning Star* (RO 85), the Rothesay-registered fishing smack, and the rowing boat named *Rose* are watched wistfully by our two young would-be navigators. Today the old stone pier has been restored and once more adds to the attraction of Kilchattan, but a bungalow now stands on the site of a small (two buses) garage, closed many years ago by Western SMT and which housed the early first bus from the village to Rothesay.

Over the years, most of the tourist traffic arriving at Rothesay has sailed by steamer from Wemyss Bay. Another way to reach the island, however, is by ferry from Colintraive over the narrows of the Kyles of Bute to Rhubodach. Although this is a centuries old ferry crossing, it has only been since 1950 that a vehicle ferry has operated, initially a former tank landing craft. Today, one can travel between Dunoon and Rothesay by means of the bus connections provided by West Coast Motors, requiring no change of transport as the bus crosses on board. To anyone from the Glasgow area this makes a splendid day out leaving the car at home. Take the train to Gourock, ferry to Dunoon, thence the scenic bus journey to Rothesay, return by ferry to Wemyss Bay and train home. This is a recommended example of many such connections (which can equally be enjoyed in the opposite direction) now available on the Clyde Coast which sadly are largely underused. Here we see Plaxton Beaver-bodied Mercedes-Benz Vario SF06 ODT of West Coast Motors leaving the ferry *Loch Dunvegan* at Rhubodach during summer 2009 to continue down the eastern shore of Bute via Port Bannatyne to Rothesay.

How did the buses reach Bute before the days of the car ferries which were introduced on the Rothesay run in 1955? In pre-war days they travelled as deck cargo, but in the 1940s and 50s Western SMT regularly used a barge or landing craft which sailed from Greenock to Rothesay. Hector Souter, a former bus driver colleague, captured this fine shot at Greenock's Victoria Harbour during his schooldays in May 1949. It reveals what happened to a particular bus *en route* to the island when both barge and bus sank in the harbour. Fortunately both were salvaged and AG 8257, a 1932 Leyland Titan continued after drying out to serve in Western's Rothesay fleet until 1952. The foremost vessel in the harbour was the support craft used by the divers who carried out the rescue mission.

Typical of the paddle steamers which over the decades delivered thousands of happy holidaymakers to Rothesay, this scene from around 1947 shows Denny-built *Caledonia* of 1934 beyond the pier buildings, while in the foreground is *Talisman* of 1935. *Talisman* was built by A & J Inglis Ltd. and is of particular interest since she was the first direct drive diesel-electric paddle steamer in the world. For several post-war years she served the Craigendoran connection from Rothesay. Also just visible in this view is the canvas roof of one of the Tilling Stevens buses owned by Rothesay Tramways.

The Pier, Rothesay

A few years later, in the early 1950s, Western SMT operated a variety of mainly secondhand buses at Rothesay, where they had absorbed the tramways business at the end of 1949. Across the quiet waters of the harbour on a misty morning is one of several Leyland Titans which had originally operated in the early 1930s with SMT in Ayr. Rothesay Depot tended to receive buses from other areas of the Western empire towards the end of their lives. High standards of maintenance and cleanliness at Pointhouse meant that Bute-based buses nevertheless had a high level of presentation.

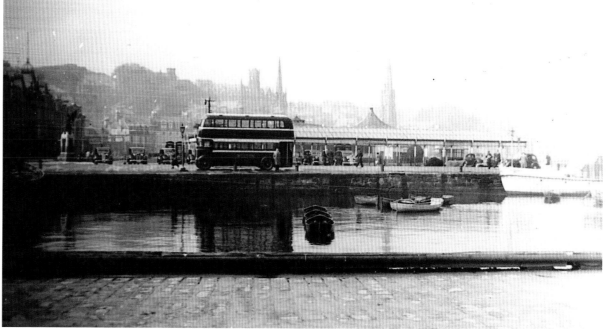

After a period with Stagecoach, Bute's bus services are now in the control of West Coast Motors. Although there is not the same demand for tours as formerly, for the benefit of holidaymakers and day trippers alike, an enjoyable island excursion by open-top double decker runs daily during the summer season. Car ferry *Bute* has just arrived from Wemyss Bay, hopefully bringing custom for former London Transport Leyland Titan B79 WUV of 1984.

It was still possible in the 1950s to see horse-drawn landaus lined up along with the taxis at the pierhead in Millport to meet incoming visitors from the steamers. I am told the last one survived until the early 1960s, operated by the MacGillivray Arms Hotel in Stuart Street. This scene from the late 1940s shows a couple of elderly open Austin hackney cars and a horse landau awaiting custom. We are reminded of the days when many shops could pull out their blinds above the premises to stop the sun from fading the window displays, as witnessed by most of the local shops along the front.

Before Cumbrae Slip opened to accommodate car ferries, the island was reached using a former Thames ferry renamed *Keppel* or one of the '*Maid*' class from Largs to Millport. Excursion steamers also called at Millport, and looking down Cardiff Street past the various cycle hiring establishments towards the Old Pier in 1969, we see the paddle steamer *Waverley*. She had arrived from Craigendoran and would be sailing shortly for Rothesay and Tighnabruaich. Passenger transport was solely owned by Millport Motors in those pre-Cumbrae Slip days, and included a Ford Transit on the service to the caravan park and golf course lying above the town. A former W Alexander Bedford SB/Burlingham Seagull, one of a pair still in Alexander's blue livery, also connected with the few sailings which still called at Keppel Pier. Two ex-Kyle of Lochalsh ferries, *Coruisk* and *Largs* (originally *Kyleakin*) started the new route to Cumbrae Slip in 1972, and were replaced by the larger *Isle of Cumbrae* in 1977. Ever-increasing traffic justified the replacement of *Isle of Cumbrae* in 1986 with two new ferries, *Loch Striven* and *Loch Linnhe,* allocated to the Largs – Cumbrae crossing.

Cumbrae today is a peaceful place, where its bikes and buses co-exist comfortably on the twelve mile circular coastal road which hugs the island shoreline. For a period in the 1980s, however, the situation was definitely different. De-regulation of bus services had taken place in 1986 and Cumbrae's then sole operator, Morrison's Millport Motors, experienced competition from local garage proprietor Sandy Wright who took advantage of the more relaxed legislation by starting a copycat service known as Cumbrae Coaches. No holds barred rivalry saw drivers racing each other to and from Cumbrae Slip and the cyclists necessarily had to exercise greater caution, many confining themselves to the west side road which was not used by the service buses. This typical reminder of those times shows three buses awaiting custom at Cumbrae Slip in 1987 from the approaching CalMac ferry *Loch Linnhe* when one would normally have been sufficient. From the left, these were Leyland National GGE 169T and Duple-bodied Leyland Leopard BHO 7R of Millport Motors, with ECW-bodied Bristol RE UEL 566J of Cumbrae Coaches.

Both companies still survive today, but in harmony. No more racing, and ticket sharing has been introduced. Dennis Dart N804 GRV of Millport Motors shares departure with former Crosville Leyland National GMB 388T of Cumbrae Coaches. Each September, Cumbrae's Country and Western Festival takes place in Millport and Cumbrae Coaches have accordingly entered fully into the spirit of things!

At the Millport end of the run, the service terminates at the pierhead. In 1989 Millport Motors' former Strathclyde Buses Leyland National GGE 173T shares the small stance with former Crosville Bristol RE HFM 194J of Cumbrae Coaches.

Although horse-drawn carriage tours and motor charabanc excursions ran in pre-war days from Millport around the Great Cumbrae, these lapsed for many years until in 1999 Stagecoach arrived and re-invented them. An open-top double decker was used and in this scene at Fintry Bay Tearoom on the island's west side we see 1984 Leyland Olympian B81 WUV in service during the first season in 1999. This side of Cumbrae is not served by the local buses to and from the ferry slip and as such is more popular with the many cyclists who regard a day in Millport as incomplete without hiring a bike from Bremners, Mapes or Martins. Despite persevering each season until 2002 the Cumbrae Open Top Experience as it was called did not justify continuance and has not operated since.

Brodick Bustle

Arrival at Arran meant Brodick for most, indeed after closure of Lochranza Pier in 1971 there was no remaining option if travelling from the central belt. *Duchess of Hamilton* makes an impressive entry to the island in August 1969 as she bears down on Brodick Pier. Arran Transport's connecting SHO 801, a Duple(Midland)-bodied AEC Reliance of 1957 originally with Liss & District of Bordon, will shortly show 'Whiting Bay' and return there fully loaded with passengers from the boat. The venerable '*Duchess*' had only one further season in service before retiring after almost forty years on the Clyde.

GOUROCK—DUNOON

Passage time—20 minutes

Leaving GOUROCK		Leaving DUNOON	
WEEK-DAYS		WEEK-DAYS	
06 50	15 20	07 30	16 10
08 00	16 55	08 35	17 30C
09 20	18 05C	10 10	17 40F
10 55	18 30F	11 35	18 40B
12 15	19 55A	13 10	19 10D
14 00		14 40	20 35A
SUNDAYS		SUNDAYS	
09 20	15 20	10 10	16 10
10 55	16 50	11 35	17 30
12 15	18 15	13 10	19 00
14 00	19 50	14 40	20 35

WEMYSS BAY—ROTHESAY

Passage Time—30 minutes

Leaving WEMYSS BAY		Leaving ROTHESAY	
WEEK-DAYS		WEEK-DAYS	
07 45	17 45SO	06 50	16 50
09 45	18 15SX	08 50	18 50SO
11 45	19 45SO	10 50	1950SXG
13 45SO	20 30SXG	12 50	20 30SO
15 45		14 50SO	
SUNDAYS		SUNDAYS	
09 45	15 45	10 50	16 50
11 45	17 45	12 50	18 50
13 45	19 40	14 50	

FAIRLIE—ARRAN (Brodick)

Passage Time—65 minutes

27 May to 30 September

Leaving FAIRLIE	Leaving BRODICK
WEEK-DAYS	WEEK-DAYS
06 55	19 00SO
	19 20SX
SUNDAYS	SUNDAYS
11 00K	16 45K

16 April to 26 May

Leaving FAIRLIE		Leaving BRODICK	
WEEK-DAYS		WEEK-DAYS	
06 55MX	11 10SX	06 45MO	16 00
08 00MO	17 30SO	08 35SO	19 25H
10 25SO	18 10H	09 30SX	
No Service on Sundays		No service on Sundays	

A Mons, Fris and Sats only until 6 May, daily from 8 May
B Until 6 May   C Until 26 May   D From 8 May
F From 27 May   G Mons and Fris only until 5 May Daily
(except Sats) from 8 May H 8 and 26 May only
K 11 June to 10 September.   MO Mons only.
MX Mons excepted.   SO Sats only.   SX Sats excepted.

WEMYSS BAY—MILLPORT
Particulars on application

ARDROSSAN—ARRAN (Brodick)
Winton Pier

Passage Time—50 minutes

27 May to 30 September

Leaving ARDROSSAN		Leaving BRODICK	
WEEK-DAYS		WEEK-DAYS	
10 20	17 30SO	08 35	16 30SX
14 15	18 00SX	12 20	
		16 00SO	
No Service on Sundays		No Service on Sundays	

CHARGES
For accompanying motor cars (including driver)

GOUROCK—DUNOON

Overall length of Car	SINGLE	RETURN
Not exceeding 11 feet	17/-	25/-
Not exceeding 13 feet	20/-	30/-
Not exceeding 14 feet 6 inches	26/-	38/-
Exceeding 14 feet 6 inches	30/-	45/-

WEMYSS BAY—ROTHESAY or MILLPORT

	SINGLE	RETURN
Not exceeding 11 feet	24/-	36/-
Not exceeding 13 feet	29/-	44/-
Not exceeding 14 feet 6 inches	35/-	51/-
Exceeding 14 feet 6 inches	42/-	60/-

FAIRLIE or ARDROSSAN—BRODICK

	SINGLE	RETURN
Not exceeding 11 feet	48/-	72/-
Not exceeding 13 feet	56/-	84/-
Not exceeding 14 feet 6 inches	77/-	114/-
Exceeding 14 feet 6 inches	96/-	145/-

CIRCLE FARE
Gourock to Dunoon, and Rothesay to Wemyss Bay, or in reverse direction—

Not exceeding 11 feet	29/-
Not exceeding 13 feet	33/-
Not exceeding 14 feet 6 inches	41/-
Exceeding 14 feet 6 inches	48/-

Pier dues are payable at Dunoon, Rothesay, Millport and Brodick.

Passenger accommodation on car carrying vessels includes lounge, tearoom and fully licensed smokeroom bar.

PASSENGER RETURN FARES

Gourock-Dunoon 7/6	Wemyss Bay-Rothesay 9/3
Wemyss Bay—Millport	9/3
Ardrossan/Fairlie—Brodick	14/-

Cars must be available for shipment 15 minutes before advertised time of departure. **It is advisable for motorists to reserve shipping space prior to date of travel.** Motor car and passenger tickets issued at the Purser's Office on board vessels.

Drive on Drive off

clyde car ferry services

Gourock - Dunoon
Wemyss Bay - Rothesay
Fairlie Pier - Brodick
Ardrossan - Brodick
Wemyss Bay - Millport

16 April to 30 September 1967

THE CALEDONIAN STEAM PACKET CO. LTD.

Largely thanks to the immediate popularity of the 'ABC' general purpose car ferries on the upper Clyde sailings (*Arran, Bute* and *Cowal*) in the mid-1950s a fourth vessel was commissioned by the Caledonian Steam Packet. This was *Glen Sannox*, built at the Ailsa yard in Troon and which started on the Arran run in 1957, with the same success as had been experienced in Dunoon and Rothesay. Timetable alterations were obviously required and the Arran bus connections to and from Brodick were necessarily 'tweaked' to suit the new ferry timings but this was implemented smoothly and satisfactorily. Connecting coach tours on the island were normally publicised in the steamer publicity, as were the connecting service buses, even including the names of the operators in earlier editions of the timetable.

Brodick Pier was always busy at steamer time, not least on the arrival of the mid-morning sailing from Ardrossan when hundreds of day trippers would pour from the *Glen Sannox*. Many would make their way to the awaiting colourful assortment of local buses destined for all parts of Scotland's holiday isle. These scenes illustrate the atmosphere on a summer's day in 1963 – June 1st to be exact – when the weather was warm, the sky was blue and the buses were just about any colour you might wish.

The lull before the storm. Within five minutes, however, the pier will be pulsating once *Glen Sannox*, seen approaching over the bay, ties up. Bannatyne Motors of Blackwaterfoot operated this 1949 Brockhouse-bodied Maudslay originally owned by Youngs' Bus Service of Paisley and later acquired by Western SMT. The destination was Corriecravie, a service previously operated by Stewart's Motors of that village and the route was via Lamlash, Whiting Bay and Kildonan although Bannatyne also operated direct to Blackwaterfoot via the cross-island String Road.

The 'Sannox' has sailed in from Ardrossan and suddenly the pier has sprung to life. All adding to the Brodick bustle, holidaymakers and day trippers seek out 'their' bus amongst the almost bewildering choice. Duplication was often necessary on busier days. On this occasion the selection included Commer, Albion, AEC and Leyland vehicles, owned by Ribbeck of Brodick and Lennox of Whiting Bay.

There was no mistaking the blue and cream colours of E.K. Ribbeck of Brodick. Commer/Plaxton SJ 1189 of 1948 leaves loaded for Lochranza, but is duplicated by Albion/Duple CHH 740 (which can be seen in the centre of the previous picture), also dating from 1948 and possibly my own favourite Arran bus as a young enthusiast. I loved that traditional radiator and was also fascinated by the fact that it boasted two gear levers! One was for boosting into overdrive.

Lennox loads up for Whiting Bay. The long-established A.C. Lennox & Sons operated most journeys on the busy Brodick – Lamlash – Whiting Bay route, linking Arran's most populous villages. SJ 1261 was a 1949 Commer with bodywork by Scottish Aviation of Prestwick Airport. Such a variety of vehicles (and vessels in earlier years) meant Arran was paradise for a transport enthusiast. So many different makes of chassis and bodybuilders contributed to an exceptionally interesting island.

Weir of Machrie operated to Pirnmill on the island's west coast. DBN 627, a 1949 Bedford OB/Duple will shortly be put through its paces on the steep climb over the String Road through central Arran. Over the bay, Arran's highest peak, Goatfell, gazes down at the gathering on the pier.

Only a decade earlier at Brodick there were distinct differences, no car ferry being the main one. Arran was certainly a quieter place until the arrival of the '*Sannox*' in 1957 and with it an immediate increase in vehicles and visitors alike. One can sense what I mean from these early 1950s scenes which convey the impression of a more leisurely island.

Bannatyne's Bedford from Blackwaterfoot has brought customers across the island to join the mainland steamer at Brodick. FGD 203 was a 1947 OB model with coachwork by SMT of Edinburgh to Duple design which had originally operated with Northern Roadways of Glasgow. Raincoats were necessary accessories on this wet morning as the passengers queued to pay their pier dues and purchase tickets. As always on Arran, the silent sentinel of Goatfell broods across the bay.

The puffer *Cretan* loads logs from a local lorry while two Bedfords at the pier rest beween runs. These are Weir's Duple-bodied SJ 1042 of 1946 and Ribbeck's SJ 1113, a Mulliner-bodied example of 1947.

Marchioness of Graham has arrived from Ardrossan and her passengers disembark to join the awaiting buses at Brodick. Weir of Machrie owned BYS 36 in the foreground, a 1938 Duple-bodied Bedford WTB and Bedford/Duple SJ 1042 of 1946, both bound for the west coast. Two of Bannatyne's Bedfords are also in evidence.

SJ 1298 was a Plaxton-bodied Commer Avenger purchased by Ribbeck and mainly used for tours of the island. In this 1953 view it has just passed Brodick Pier where *Marchioness of Graham* has arrived from the mainland.

Lennox of Whiting Bay owned SJ 1028, a wartime Duple utility Bedford OWB of 1944, seen on the quiet shore road in Brodick on service to Lamlash and Whiting Bay.

Brodick was not the only island village to enjoy a mainland link. Whiting Bay is captured on camera in August 1950 as the turbine steamer *Glen Sannox* of 1925 steams towards the pier. She spent most of her life as the regular vessel between Ardrossan and Arran until withdrawal in 1954. Providing the connections to the south end of the island are the two wartime utility Bedfords seen at the pierhead. These were owned by Gordon Bros. of Lamlash and with their wooden slatted seats must at least have made an impression on their passengers. The hire cars were mainly owned by Lennox, whose garage lay behind the photographer a little way up the hill. Currie's lorry is also visible heading down the pier to collect trunks and luggage for delivery to local holiday homes. This illustrates what was usually the busiest steamer arrival of the day, when the 10.15 a.m. sailing from Ardrossan reached Whiting Bay at 12.10, having called at Brodick at 11.10 and Lamlash at 11.45. After about ten minutes of great activity, Whiting Bay returned to its usual repose.

Going back to the 1920s, this was the scene which greeted incoming passengers from the steamer at Whiting Bay, with taxis available to transport customers to their holiday homes and boarding houses. Most of these vehicles were owned by the stout gentleman in flat cap and bow tie, in conversation with a driver. This was 'Pa' Lennox, boss of what was probably Arran's most important transport business.

118

Lennox's Pier Garage at Whiting Bay was, as the name suggests, a little way up the rise opposite the pier and opened in 1924 when this photo was taken to mark the occasion. Some of the drivers from the hire fleet are with 'their' respective vehicles and mostly wearing white-topped uniform caps. The cars include Minerva and Buick makes, while a small 14 seat Fiat charabanc is on the extreme right. Unusually, 'Pa' Lennox, who was not known to be shy of publicity, is not in the forefront but stands in his trademark bow tie and bunnet at the office door.

119

"ATALANTA" ARRIVING AT WHITING BAY.

Seen from above the village in the mid-1930s, this view gives a better idea of the length of Whiting Bay Pier. Two Albion buses for the south end await arrival of the approaching LMS steamer which is the John Brown-built *Atalanta* of 1906, nearing the end of her Clyde career as she was sold in 1937. Whiting Bay was home to one of the newer piers on the Firth, albeit erected in 1899. Before this a small ferry sailed across the shallow waters of the bay to meet incoming steamers as took place in other Arran villages without piers. Because of these shoals the new pier held the distinction of being the longest on the Clyde. It was finally abandoned in 1962.

Arran's west coast communities did not benefit from steamer piers like their eastern neighbours. Accordingly folks from villages such as Blackwaterfoot, Machrie and Pirnmill were disadvantaged to a degree when required to reach the mainland. This meant travelling by local bus to either Brodick or Lochranza to make the connection. There was admittedly an option for those in the Pirnmill area, but not one which necessarily appealed to everyone. This involved rowing out in a small boat to connect with the Campbeltown/Glasgow steamer which would lie offshore during the procedure as seen in this view from 1905 at Pirnmill. Edwardian ladies in all their finery watch a flotilla of rowing boats ferrying passengers to and from Williamson's turbine steamer *Queen Alexandra* on her way to Campbeltown. She was the first vessel of this name, built by Denny of Dumbarton in 1902 and enjoyed only a comparatively short life on the Clyde. She was sold in 1911 to the Canadian Pacific Railway for operation in Vancouver where she sailed until 1937 under the new name *Princess Patricia*. A replacement *Queen Alexandra* appeared on the Clyde in 1912.

Three similar cargo and passenger vessels, *Davaar*, *Kinloch* and *Kintyre* maintained a service from Victorian times for the imposingly titled Campbeltown and Glasgow Steam Packet Joint Stock Co. Ltd., between Campbeltown and Glasgow via the Kilbrannan Sound and Carradale. Here we see *Kinloch* departing Pirnmill with the familiar farewells from those on the shore. This link for goods and passengers ended in 1940 when *Davaar* was withdrawn, severing what had been a long connection for the folk of west Arran and Carradale in Kintyre.

737/13

A close-up of rowing boats linking between the Pirnmill shore and the steamer waiting out in the waters of Kilbrannan Sound, which is not visible here. This Edwardian scene possibly explains the reluctance of many to travel this way; unsteady planking, slippery seaweed, and small overcrowded boats low in the water all conspired against this mode of travel. It was possibly okay on a calm, dry day but when wet and windy I suspect I would have opted to join the horse-drawn carriage (or later, bus) to Lochranza or across the island to Brodick, there connecting with the mainland boat.

No transport in this picture but it shows one of the major attractions for many who came to Arran and is equally popular today. Golf has always been one of the main links encouraging visitors to the island. 'Gowff' as it was still known in Victorian times was born here in Scotland and where better than Scotland's holiday isle to perfect your swing, with a selection of courses to tempt? In the days when steamers connected with many parts of the island, golf was often a reason for booking a holiday in a specific village, where many returned faithfully year on year. Pirnmill was a typical example and here we see Edwardian ladies and gentlemen concentrating on a putt at the fourth tee of Pirnmill Links.

A particularly good selection of picture postcards of the Pirnmill area was available in earlier years, largely due to entrepreneur Robert Anderson. Originally the local blacksmith, he (and later his son John) not only ran the village shop and tearoom but was also a proficient amateur photographer who published his own local view cards. Additionally he operated the motor charabanc service between Pirnmill, Catacol and Lochranza. This was used by all those who disliked the thought of the short but nonetheless exposed trip by rowing boat to or from the steamer at pierless Pirnmill. From the shore outside Anderson's tearoom we look across Kilbrannan Sound to the Kintyre coast and parked in the foreground is the hiring fleet of 1926. Prominent is SN 2055, a 1923 Austin behind which is GD 2186, a brand new French-built Berliet charabanc and GB 9589, an American Buick of 1925. Beyond the Austin is SJ 439, a Model T Ford chara of 1924, used along with the Berliet for the connection to Catacol and Lochranza.

A similar situation to that at Pirnmill took place at Machrie Bay, which at least boasted what passed as a pier giving extra confidence to prospective passengers. This Edwardian scene looks across Kilbrannan Sound towards the Carradale coast and was taken by Peter Weir of a well-known local family.

Davaar was Clyde-built in 1885 by the London & Glasgow Iron Shipbuilding Co. Ltd. She arrives at Lochranza around 1905 where no doubt a number of Pirnmill passengers would disembark to join a carriage for the remainder of their journey rather than experience the ritual of the rowing boat. Note the pier bell which was used as a warning signal in foggy weather.

On page 121 we see the original *Queen Alexandra* at Pirnmill. Here is her Denny-built replacement and namesake during her initial season in 1912 approaching the pier at Lochranza. Amongst the group waiting to welcome the incoming passengers are two small boys in sailor suits, a style now fallen firmly from favour, likewise the big hats and long skirts of their female relatives. *Queen Alexandra* became *Saint Columba* on acquisition by David MacBrayne in 1935 and received a third funnel. She sailed majestically on until the end of the 1958 season.

Lying at the ferry slip beside the remains of the old pier at Lochranza is the car ferry of the same name which was built specially for the Claonaig crossing in 1987. Parked at the pierhead to uplift passengers from Kintyre is Western Scottish Hestair Duple 425 coach LH106 (VLT 206) which will proceed to the Kinloch Hotel at Blackwaterfoot.

In the 1920s and 30s John Currie of Shiskine provided an alternative for those who wished to avoid a possible soaking in a small boat. Boarding for Brodick and steamer connection to the mainland is Currie's SJ 688, an Albion PD41 type with canvas-roofed coachwork by Stewart of Wishaw and finished in an attractive blue livery. The location is the Kinloch Hotel at Blackwaterfoot, still the bus terminus today. Suitcases are loaded at the rear, with the conductor giving instructions through the open roof. Nevertheless, one passenger prefers to take care of his own and strides purposefully with suitcase and golf bag to board the bus. In 1940 Currie sold his business to Ribbeck of Brodick.

Scenes at the Arran end of the sailing always seem more prevalent than on the mainland at Ardrossan, which shall now be remedied! *Glen Sannox* of 1957 is busy loading vehicles for Brodick at Winton Pier while the connecting three car Derby class diesel multiple unit, forming part of a six car train, waits in the adjacent station.

BRITISH RAILWAYS
WINTON PIER STATION

Left: Not only did the small boat procedure take place on Arran's west coast but also at both King's Cross and Corrie on the east. Viewed from Corrie in 1923, we see a laden ferry boat leaving *Duchess of Rothesay* which had sailed from Greenock to Arran via the Kyles of Bute. The almost obligatory onlookers share sandwiches on the shore as they enjoy one of the highlights of life in Corrie in the 'twenties.

Below: An earlier scene from around 1900 and unusual in that it looks from the water towards the ferry landing place at Corrie and judging by the numbers scrambling up the shore path, a steamer has recently arrived.

Left: King's Cross was a further example of a village where passengers were rowed from the shore to join steamers. Despite lying only a short distance from the main road between Lamlash and Whiting Bay, King's Cross has largely been denied bus coverage since the regular service buses do not divert through. In the 1920s local carrier John Kerr of Dalghorm, Lamlash, provided the connection between his home village and King's Cross for both goods and passengers, using this open wagonette. This was SJ 222, a GMC dating from 1920 and painted green. It was later sold to Ernest Bolt of Lamlash who continued the run for a while.

Leaving a broad wake astern as she sets sail from Brodick, *Caledonia* sweeps away from the pier and round the bay under the ever watchful gaze of Goatfell.

"Bye, bye, Arran"

Leaving Arran and sailing on down the Firth, we next tie up at Campbeltown. I arrived here for the first time in 1958, accompanied by a fond aunt and uncle, on board *Duchess of Hamilton* on the popular four and a quarter hour long cruise from Gourock which allowed an hour and twenty five minutes in the 'Wee Toon'. "More than enough" I hear some say but even if Campbeltown had little appeal for a few, then there were connections providing a quick tour across Kintyre to Machrihanish by McConnachie's bus or down to Southend with West Coast Motors. If you had arrived by 1931, it was also possible to travel by narrow gauge steam train to Machrihanish, whose timings also connected with the steamers. This line closed that season, hastened by severe competition from McConnachie's bus and must be one of the earliest examples of this taking place. Here we see the train at the Campbeltown terminus hauled by locomotive *Argyll*, an 0-6-2 tank engine built in 1906 by Andrew Barclay at Kilmarnock.

THE PIER AND HARBOUR, CAMPBELTOWN, ARGYLL   B 3086

The usual group of retired local men in dark suits and bunnets, probably mainly fishermen, watch the crowds walk back to rejoin *Marchioness of Graham* and *Duchess of Hamilton* during the summer of 1950.

Right: David MacBrayne was granted a licence in 1940 to operate its own bus as a substitute connection between Glasgow and Campbeltown after withdrawal of the Clyde and Campbeltown Shipping Company steamer via west Arran and Carradale. This 140 mile journey left the city at 3.15 p.m. arriving in the 'Wee Toon' at 8.40 p.m. where bus and crew stayed overnight prior to returning to Glasgow at 7 a.m. These were MacBrayne's only through journeys between Campbeltown and Glasgow for many years.

Above: West Coast Motors and A. & P. McConnachie both provided connections between Campbeltown and Tarbert, the 'Wee Toon''s rival village at the top end of Kintyre. West Coast ran not only on the main road up the west side of the peninsula but also on certain days via the indifferent east side road via Carradale and Grogport. It was McConnachie, however, who provided the official link with the MacBrayne bus for Glasgow-bound passengers or points *en route*. At Tarbert Harbour in 1962 is McConnachie's grey and blue SB 8250, an impressive Leyland Royal Tiger of 1950 with unusual Duple Roadmaster bodywork identical to a popular Dinky Toy of the time. The road trip to Campbeltown was a leisurely business, leaving MacBrayne's Parliamentary Road coach station at 9 a.m. and arriving Tarbert at 1.05 p.m. when one had time for lunch before continuing with McConnachie at 2.15 p.m. and eventually arriving at Campbeltown around 4 p.m.

Passenger Plane at Bridgend, Islay.

Photo. CAMERON, BOWMORE

Although Campbeltown lost its rail link to Machrihanish in 1931, only two years later it gained a much more important connection, this time by air. In April 1933, Midland & Scottish Air Ferries Ltd., the fledgling airline owned by far-sighted entrepreneur John Sword, general manager of the Western SMT bus company, made its initial passenger and freight landing at the old Strath Airfield on the Laggan. The flights originated at Glasgow (Renfrew Aerodrome) and linked the city with Kintyre and Islay, where initially planes touched down on the strand at Bridgend, as they still do on Barra. A later move was made to Glenegedale Airport on Islay by which time Scottish Airways controlled the operation. This view shows one of the early Midland flights on the beach at Bridgend after arrival from Campbeltown. 'Midland' had also been the fleetname of Sword's own bus company which was acquired by the SMT group in 1932. The plane is a DH 84 Dragon registered in 1933 as G-ACCZ.

Let's take the bus from Campbeltown up through the Kintyre Peninsula to Tarbert. The route takes us by the main road along the west coast, calling *en route* at Tayinloan where a further connection is available by CalMac ferry to the Island of Gigha. For a short period in 1995 it was possible to make this journey without changing as Essbee Buses, who had gained some of the Campbeltown area bus operations under tender, provided a direct Campbeltown – Gigha service via the ferry on Saturdays, their bus crossing on board. Wadham Stringer-bodied Mercedes M89 EGE is seen on this service at Gigha Hotel.

The final season of transport operation by McConnachie of Campbeltown was summer 1970 after which the business was sold to West Coast Motors, their former rivals from the 'Wee Toon'. This view at Tarbert Harbour shows two of McConnachie's final purchases prior to the demise. CSB 441-2D were both Plaxton-bodied Bedford VAM5s which had been new to Gold Line of Dunoon in 1966 and still in the livery of their former owner. Also visible are two MacBrayne AEC Reliances providing the onward link to Glasgow.

Above: Commodore Captain Angus McKinnon, master of MacBrayne's R.M.S. *Saint Columba* personally supervises a speed-up of cargo discharge at Tarbert on arrival from Gourock in 1958. Every second counted towards punctuality, especially during the summer season, as an extra leg of the journey extended the sailing up Loch Fyne to Ardrishaig, with only a brief turnaround before heading home. An amazing variety of items await collection, from a buggy to bread from UCBS (the Co-op bakery), suitcases to sausages and from cakes to what looks suspiciously like a coffin.

Left: A large pile of mailbags sits on the East Loch Pier at Tarbert in 1965. They have arrived from Lochgilphead on board MacBrayne's Bedford/Duple (Midland) WGG 623, seen on the right. On arrival of the steamer this bus will depart for Lochgilphead where a further connection will be made with MacBrayne's Oban bus. The Glasgow-bound bus is AEC Reliance 45 (WGG 634) which would have left Tarbert at 2.30 p.m. arriving in the city at 6.45 p.m.

At the other end of the short but important inter-loch connection at Tarbert, West Coast Motors Bedford/Duple SB 8280 awaits passengers from Islay disembarking MacBrayne's *Locheil* at the West Loch.

We can either sail from Tarbert aboard the mail steamer on the final leg of her journey from Gourock to Ardrishaig, or catch MacBrayne's bus. Let's imagine we've sailed and the year is 1935. The hands of the clock on the pier buildings at Ardrishaig indicate ten past one, signifying departure time for R.M.S. *Columba* to Gourock and Glasgow in those days. She is visible behind the buses which provided connections for Oban, Glasgow and Tarbert. On the left are two Maudslays, with an AEC Regal to the right, painted in MacBrayne's rich red and cream livery of the time, prior to the introduction of green. This was the final season of *Columba's* sailings as she was then withdrawn after an incredible 58 years on the Clyde, having been launched at Thomson's Clydebank yard in April 1878 and operating the famous 7.11 a.m. departure from Glasgow for so long.

Also at Ardrishaig is MacBrayne's road connection to Inveraray which supplemented the through bus to Glasgow and was always known as the 'Inveraray Mail'. A smaller type of bus was allocated to this service, in this instance 42 (SB 3832), a 20 seat Bedford WLG type of 1931 bodied by Bracebridge of Lincoln. Note the stairs leading to the rooftop luggage hopper which would be utilised when the driver attended to the waiting passengers whose luggage awaits him on the pier.

For those who were not the world's best sailors, the introduction of a through bus service from Glasgow to Argyllshire via the 'Rest and Be Thankful' proved a boon. This was pioneered not by MacBrayne but by the appropriately named Link Lines Ltd., a Glasgow firm largely owned by the India Tyre Company and based in the city at Clyde Street. Starting in April 1927 the service proved immediately successful. Needless to say, MacBrayne felt the chill, particularly with a decline in passenger numbers on the *Columba* and decided to introduce their own rival service, which started in August 1929. Apparently the Loch Fyneside folk remained largely faithful to the original operator and continued to favour Link Lines but perhaps inevitably the larger company eventually triumphed and in 1932 took over the Link business. Their fleet of Leyland Tigers and Crossleys was only partially retained for MacBrayne service. GE 5608 was one of Link's 1929 Leylands with bodywork by Midland of Airdrie. One of its destination bills reads 'Dunoon' which was a further connection provided by the company, linking at Cairndow, but was not continued by MacBrayne.

After shipping movements at West Loch Tarbert Pier ended in 1979 the Islay sailings operated from deeper water down the loch at Kennacraig. In July 1999 CalMac's 1984 vessel *Isle of Arran* has brought custom to Mercedes F77 HAU of Henderson Hiring, Tarbert, making the connection to Skipness. In 2006 Henderson sold the business to an expanding West Coast Motors.